Growth of Soci

Unemployment Insurance	Health Insurance	[Family Allowances &] Compensation
1911 National Insurance Act (Part 2) applied to selected trades only	1911 National Insurance Act (Part I) applied to low-paid workers	1906 Workmen's Compensation extended to most occupations
1920 Unemployment Insurance extended to most workers		1923 Workmen's Compensation further extended
1921 Dependants' Allowances. 'Extended benefits' allowed		
1946 National Insurance Act applied to all citizens of working age. Benefits for 'interruption of earnings' due to sickness, unemployment or old age		1945 Family Allowances Act 1946 Industrial Injuries Act (Workmen's Compensation replaced by new scheme)
	1948 National Health Service—free to all	
1966 Wage-related Short-term Benefits 1975 Earnings Related National Insurance		1971 Family Income Supplement 1977 Child Benefit

The Making of
the Welfare State

Second Edition

R. J. Cootes M.A.

LONGMAN

Longman Group Limited,
Longman House, Burnt Mill, Harlow, Essex CM20 2JE, England
and Associated Companies throughout the World.

First published 1966
Second edition 1984

ISBN 0 582 22362 8

Set in 11/12 Linotron Baskerville

**Printed in Hong Kong by
Wilture Printing Co. Ltd.**

Acknowledgements

We are grateful to the following for permission to reproduce photographs:
BBC Hulton Picture Library, pages 6, 7, 9, 13, 14, 16, 18, 20, 22, 26, 30, 35,
37, 38, 40, 43, 45, 49, 50, 52, 54, 56, 58, 59, 61, 70, 73, 74, 76, 80, 84, 85, 86,
94, 95, 97, 99, 101, 104, 107, 108, 111; British Library, page 11; BUPA, page
125; City Engineer and Surveyors Department, York, page 67; George
Clark, page 123; Controller of Her Majesty's Stationery Office, page 128;
Daily Mirror, page 83; Department of Health and Social Security, leaflet
SB.1, Nov. 82, front page, page 122; Greater London Council Photograph
Library, page 25 (2); Cartoon by David Low reproduced by permission of
The Standard, page 78; National Portrait Gallery, pages 4, 12; F. O'Brien,
page 133; The Open University, Milton Keynes, page 130; Popperfoto,
pages 29, 92; *Punch*, pages 39, 47, 88, 102, 109, 120; Rowntree Mackintosh
Archives, page 63; Shelter, page 127; Topham, page 116; WRVS, page 131;
North Yorkshire County Library, Copyright: Northern Echo, North of England Newspapers (Westminster Press Ltd) Priestgate, Darlington, pages 65,
118.

Contents

Introduction

The Meaning of the Welfare State

Early in July 1948 the *Daily Mail* told its readers:

On Monday morning you will wake in a new Britain, in a State which 'takes over' its citizens six months before they are born, providing care and free services for their birth, for their early years, their schooling, sickness, workless days, widowhood and retirement. All this, with free doctoring, dentistry and medicine—free bathchairs, too, if needed—for 4*s.* 11*d.* (24½p) out of your weekly pay packet. You begin paying next Friday.

The great day in question was the 'Appointed Day' for the beginning of the Welfare State, 5 July, when the major social services of modern Britain came into operation.

Things like this do not happen out of the blue. The British Welfare State was created after a long struggle going back well into the last century. In this book you will be able to trace that struggle, stage by stage. It was fought by social reformers of all kinds, both inside and outside Parliament, to give ordinary people financial security in times of hardship and a greater share in the benefits of civilisation. The story of the Welfare State shows that history is not always about 'battles and great men' and that some of the most important achievements of the past are among the least spectacular.

PART ONE: 'THE TWO NATIONS'

1 'Self-Help'

Have you ever wondered what sort of life you would have had if you had been born a century earlier—in the reign of Victoria (1837–1901)? We have all read stories of great country houses where some people lived a life of leisure with countless servants and everything they wanted; but what of the ordinary working people, who were the vast majority? In an age when Britain was the most powerful country in the world, with an empire which stretched across the globe, the greatest navy and the most advanced industries, there existed, among riches and plenty for the few, millions of people living out their lives in misery and squalor.

Victorian Contrasts

Benjamin Disraeli, who later became Prime Minister, wrote a book in 1845 in which he described the rich and poor as Two Nations '. . . between whom there is no sympathy; who are as ignorant of each other's habits, thoughts and feelings as if they were dwellers in different zones, or inhabitants of different planets; who are formed by different breeding; are fed by a different food, are ordered by different manners, and are not governed by the same laws'.

In the previous year, a German reformer, Friedrich Engels, gave this vivid account of early Victorian town life: 'A horde of ragged women and children swarm about, as filthy as the swine that thrive on the garbage heaps and in the puddles . . . The race that lives in these ruinous cottages behind broken windows . . . or in dark wet cellars in measureless stench and filth . . . must really have reached the lowest stage of humanity.' Engels was not exaggerating. In Manchester at this time sixty babies out of every hundred born died before

Slum living in London in the mid-nineteenth century: this sketch shows a family of ten crowded into an attic

reaching the age of five. In Liverpool, one family in five lived in a damp, dark cellar. Cholera and other killing diseases raged in the towns—encouraged by the appalling lack of sanitation.

At the other extreme, some rich, aristocratic families lived a life of luxury and idleness. A constant round of balls and parties, hunting and shooting, cards and billiards, amateur theatricals and music-making was carried on in the great mansions of the land. These often stood in beautiful parks, and employed scores of butlers, cooks, gardeners and servants of all kinds. Mrs Stanhope, in Anthony Trollope's novel *Barchester Towers*, was far from being one of the aristocracy, yet she was typical of a 'woman of leisure' of this period: 'Her dress was always perfect; she never dressed but once in a day, and never appeared till between three and four; but when she did appear, she appeared at her best . . . her ornaments were costly, rare and such as could not fail to attract notice . . . But when we have said that Mrs Stanhope knew how to dress . . . we have said all. Other purpose in life she had none'.

3

The Victorian Age was full of such contrasts. While a woman of leisure frittered away her time, secure from the anxieties of the outside world, a woman of the labouring class worked a long day in a factory or on the land for a pittance. Babies were often taken into factories and put on the floor by the machines while their mothers worked. Children took full-time jobs as young as six or seven to help make ends meet. Even so, the likely reward for such toil was poverty and an early grave.

The Teachings of Samuel Smiles

Most well-to-do Victorians were ignorant of the way working people really lived. Many shut their eyes to the problems and simply said it was up to the poor to help themselves. They genuinely believed that it made a man spineless if he was given a helping hand—that he would always want to lean on someone else rather than stand on his own feet. This attitude was summed up by Samuel Smiles, an Edinburgh doctor, in a book called *Self-Help* (1859). He said hard work was the answer to poverty, for 'they who are the most persistent, and work in the truest spirit, will invariably be the most successful'. In a later book, called simply *Thrift* (by which he meant

Samuel Smiles—populariser of self-help

4

a careful use of money, putting some by for when it was needed), he said: 'How much of human happiness depends on the spending of the penny well . . . a penny saved is the seed of pounds saved'.

It was all very well for Samuel Smiles, along with rich industrialists and business men, to preach the people smug sermons about the virtue of self-reliance. In fact, it took ability, ambition and a large slice of luck for an unskilled labourer, with no education, to improve his position in the world. How could the working classes save money when their wages were often so low that they could not manage in a normal week? If such people struggled under normal conditions you can imagine how hard life would be for them if the family income was suddenly reduced by sickness, unemployment, old age or death. They could not afford to 'save for a rainy day', so they were totally unprepared for such a calamity. If the father of a family died, or was out of work for a long period, his wife had to carry on somehow without his wages. 'Self-help' was no answer in these circumstances.

The better paid, more highly skilled workers *could* help themselves. They could afford weekly subscriptions to a Friendly Society or a trade union, in return for which they received cash benefits in time of need. There were well over a million members of Friendly Societies by the mid-nineteenth century. For their weekly payments, members usually got an allowance during sickness, a pension in old age and a sum of money at death to help with the funeral expenses. Most of these societies were small, local organisations, but there were some large, national ones, such as the 'Hearts of Oak', established in 1841. Ordinary labourers were not admitted, however; only those earning above a certain wage were eligible.

Many trade unions provided benefits for members, in the same way as Friendly Societies, although their main purpose was to obtain improvements in wages and conditions of work. In the rules of the Amalgamated Society of Engineers, established in 1851, it stated that one of the tasks of the union was 'to promote the general and material welfare of its members, to assist them when out of work or in distressed circumstances, to support them in case of sickness, accident or superannuation (old age), and loss of tools by fire, to provide for

5

Victorian charity—a soup kitchen in the East End of London, 1867

their burial and the burial of their wives'.

So the better paid workers had something to fall back on in time of hardship. However, those who either had no trade union or could not afford any weekly payments had to manage as best they could. This might mean no fuel in winter and insufficient food and clothing. Although a good deal of charity was given by the rich to the poor, millions of people suffered unnoticed, through no fault of their own.

Looking at this state of affairs more than a century later, we naturally ask, 'Why didn't the government do something about it?' However, at that time governments did not think it was their duty to provide schemes of welfare and assistance for people who suffered hardship. They believed that so long as they kept law and order, looked after British interests abroad, organised the nation's finances and corrected only the most glaring abuses in national life, then the people would be able to look after their own affairs. Not until the end of the century was this attitude seriously challenged.

The Poor Law

Victorian governments did, however, allow one important exception to the general principle of self-help. A Poor Law Amendment Act of 1834 had set up a system of workhouses for the totally destitute. If people found themselves jobless, homeless, sick or faced with starvation, there was always the

Men breaking stones in a labour yard

workhouse to fall back on if no one else could help. It was a last resort, and not a pleasant one at that. In order to encourage people to help themselves, and to discourage idlers from trying to get free board and lodging, life in a workhouse was made less comfortable than that of the lowest class of labourer. The occupants were set to work, in return for which they received the bare minimum of food and some kind of bed. Discipline was strict: families were separated, complete silence was observed at meals, and visiting and visitors were prohibited. Not surprisingly, these places were hated and feared by the poor. Many preferred to face starvation rather than go into the workhouse.

Workhouses were paid for out of the parish rates, and the ratepayers (householders) elected local Boards of Guardians to run them. Guardians were ratepayers themselves, so they had an interest in keeping down the running costs of the workhouse. This usually meant that the food provided was just about enough to keep body and soul together. In *Oliver Twist*, the famous novel about an orphan who was born and reared in a workhouse, Charles Dickens strongly attacked the whole system. Poor Oliver had to exist on a diet of gruel (oatmeal boiled in water). Of this, 'each boy had one porringer, and no more—except on occasions of great public rejoicing, when he had two ounces and a quarter of bread besides. The bowls never wanted washing. The boys polished them with their spoons till they shone again . . .'

Victorian workhouses had a character of their own, but they were not a new idea. The first national system of poor relief dates back to the reign of the first Elizabeth, 1558–1603. 'The Acte for the Releife of the Poore' (1598) made each parish raise local taxes, or rates, for helping its poor, handicapped and destitute people. From these rates, 'Houses of Correction' were built for 'rogues and idlers', while the unemployed poor were given 'a convenient stock of materials' upon which they could work at home.

A different scheme, which came to be known as the 'Speenhamland System', began in 1795. Because of rising prices during the French wars, farm labourers' wages had become insufficient for even the necessities of life. In Berkshire, the magistrates, meeting in the parish of Speen, decided to make labourers' wages up to a basic minimum out of the local rates. The amount of relief given in each case varied according to the price of bread and the number of children in the family. This allowance system was soon adopted throughout southern England. But farmers took advantage of it to refuse necessary increases in wages—knowing their workers could get relief from the parish. Consequently, while the rates went up alarmingly, the poor labourers were humiliated by receiving part of their income in the form of parish charity.

The Poor Law Amendment Act (1834) replaced the Speenhamland System. It discouraged the able-bodied poor from applying for relief by making them enter a workhouse to get it. The aged and sick could stay in their homes. However, in practice, it was usually cheaper and more convenient for the Guardians to herd everyone together under one roof. In some places the sick were looked after by the insane in filthy workhouse infirmaries. Orphans mixed with hardened criminals and destitute mothers with prostitutes, while those who had lived respectable lives but were forced to enter the workhouse in old age were mixed with those whose poverty was due to drunkenness and vice.

Being a pauper was now a bigger disgrace than ever before. As Disraeli said, the 1834 Act 'announced to the world that in England poverty is a crime'. Not surprisingly, the numbers on poor relief dropped sharply after 1834. The authorities were delighted, for they intended the workhouses to be a

Marylebone workhouse in west London. A new ward for the homeless poor, 1867

deterrent. Nevertheless, conditions were gradually improved during the nineteenth century. Workhouse schools were introduced to help fit children for an independent life and care of the sick was made more humane. By the 1880s sick people could be admitted to poor law hospitals without being classed as paupers.

The main features of the Victorian poor law remained until well into the twentieth century. However, long before this, there was increasing pressure, from many quarters, to persuade governments to adopt a more kindly attitude towards the needy. It was clearly unfair to treat all paupers alike. People began to distinguish between 'idlers' and the 'deserving poor', and urged that special help should be given to the latter. After all, thrift and hard work were not always enough to keep a family out of poverty. A year's bad luck could destroy the careful management of a lifetime.

9

2 Parliament and Social Reform

In the nineteenth century, the government was not expected to give the 'underdog' a helping hand. If people failed to make ends meet, for any reason, it was their own business. Government interference in family life was frowned upon even though many families, forced by poverty to enter a workhouse, were broken up for ever. W. E. Gladstone, four times Prime Minister, summed up this attitude: 'Let the government labour to its uttermost . . . (the answer to) the question whether the English father is to be the father of a happy family and the centre of a united home . . . must depend on himself.' This was small comfort to a family whose father was out of work, crippled or even dead.

However, before we condemn the Victorians for their indifference to the sufferings of the poor, we should consider another, more positive, aspect of government. Although Parliament ignored *individual* hardship, it was willing to improve the dreadful working and living conditions in the new industrial towns. Things like laying drains, paving, cleansing and lighting the streets, and protecting women and children in the factories and mines, were best dealt with on a large scale by the government rather than by private individuals all going their separate ways. A great deal was achieved in this direction—so much, in fact, that Victoria's reign is often called an 'age of reform'.

Factories and Mines

The early factories, most of them making textile goods, were established in great numbers from the late eighteenth century onwards. Hundreds of workers were brought together under one roof, usually in foul, stuffy conditions amid the whirr of

Children working in a textile factory in the 1840s

machinery. In their haste to make big profits, most of the factory owners ignored the needs of their workers. Hours were long and wages low, so it was necessary for the whole family to work. Children of six or seven worked the same hours as adults—anything up to sixteen a day! Dragged from their beds in the early hours of the morning, they were often beaten to keep them awake at their work. Sometimes exhausted children fell into the machines or slept on the roadside on their way home, until they were rescued by their parents.

The plight of these factory children soon attracted the attention of reformers. Their earliest achievements—the Acts of 1802 and 1819 which restricted children's hours of work—were largely ignored by the factory owners. Not until 1833 was the first effective Factory Act passed. It barred all children under nine from textile factories and limited the hours of older children to forty-eight a week for those under thirteen and sixty-nine for 'young persons' of thirteen to eighteen. For the first time, paid inspectors were appointed to see that the law was observed. In addition, it was laid down that every factory child was to receive two hours' schooling a day, but this was difficult to enforce and often ignored.

Anthony Ashley Cooper (1801–85), seventh Earl of Shaftesbury

The importance of the 1833 Act was that it established the principle of state intervention between employers and workers to control hours and working conditions. It was the first real success for a small group of energetic reformers led by Anthony Ashley Cooper, later Lord Shaftesbury, who devoted his life to social reform. Lord Ashley was the force behind the government's appointment of a Royal Commission on Children's Employment in 1840. Two years later, the Commission reported on the condition of underground workers in the mines. The public was horrified to learn that young girls, naked to the waist, were chained to coal tubs which they dragged, on all fours, along underground passages for twelve or more hours a day. A Mines Act (1842) prohibited the employment of women and girls underground, and a minimum age of ten was fixed for the employment of boys.

The Royal Commission reported on other industries in the following year, and its findings led to another important Factory Act in 1844. Under this Act, working hours for women became subject to the same regulations as those for 'young persons' of thirteen to eighteen. The hours for children under thirteen were further reduced, to six and a half per day, and dangerous machinery had to be fenced. Ashley's great aim, a ten-hour day, was achieved for women and young persons in the mills in 1847, although it was changed to ten and a half

Woman and child drawing coal in a mine, 1842

hours in 1850. Because the work could not be carried on by men alone, this had the effect of reducing men's hours as well.

Factory owners said the limitation of hours would ruin the textile industry. Some claimed their profit was made in the last hour of the day, so that they could not afford to work a shorter time. Yet, within a few years, they had to admit that the Factory Acts actually increased output. Workers were more efficient when they were less exhausted by long hours. The remainder of the nineteenth century saw continued progress in factory reform. Earlier Acts were extended beyond textiles to apply to other industries, including workshops. Disraeli's Government further reduced hours in 1874—to a maximum of fifty-six a week (ten hours Monday to Friday and six on Saturday). Meanwhile, more factory inspectors were appointed, with wider powers, and safety regulations were tightened.

Public Health and Housing

The Factory Acts improved conditions where people worked. At least of equal importance was the question of living conditions in the industrial towns. The population of Britain doubled between 1780 and 1830, and was to double again by 1890. This caused enormous problems of overcrowding in unhealthy houses. The connection between dirt and disease was established in the nineteenth century, but improvements

13

in public health standards were held up by insufficient government powers. No one was safe from the lack of proper sanitation. Prince Albert, the Queen's husband, died in 1861 from typhoid, as a direct result of drinking impure water.

Edwin Chadwick, the First Secretary of the Poor Law Commission, revealed that a great deal of poverty was directly caused by disease and ill health. Chadwick wanted the government to take responsibility for improving sanitation. He compiled a Report on the Sanitary Condition of the Labouring Population (1842) which said:

'Disease . . . is always found in connection with damp and filth, and close and overcrowded dwellings. . . and where these circumstances are removed by drainage, proper cleansing, better ventilation . . . the frequency of such disease is abated (lessened) . . .

The annual loss of life from filth and bad ventilation is greater than the loss from death or wounds in any wars in which the country has been engaged in modern times.'

Chadwick argued that it was better to prevent poverty caused by ill health than to spend money on poor relief when the damage was done. This was certain to appeal to ratepayers. Nevertheless, it took a severe outbreak of cholera in 1847

Edwin Chadwick (1800–90), a leading sanitary reformer

to spur the Government into action. The first Public Health Act (1848) set up a Board of Health in London which could order the establishment of local boards around the country. These would have powers over necessary services like cleansing, draining and paving the streets. Nothing was compulsory, however, and when the Board of Health was disbanded, six years later, only a sixth of the population was served by local boards. Even so, opportunities had been created for local action and, where this was taken, epidemic disease was greatly reduced.

Meanwhile, Chadwick took a hand himself, experimenting with glazed earthenware pipes for making sewers. He found them much better than the brick-lined tunnels then in use. Pipes prevented blockages, and they were soon regarded as essential for all sanitary engineering. Chadwick continually stressed the need for greater government powers if really large-scale improvements were to be achieved. However, many ratepayers were opposed to any form of centralised control. Not until 1871, with the formation of the Local Government Board, was there an effective central authority to co-ordinate all sanitary, public health and poor law services throughout the country.

The climax of mid-Victorian concern with sanitation was the 1875 Public Health Act, passed during Disraeli's Ministry. It set up a uniform service of sanitary authorities throughout the whole country. They were responsible for sewerage, water supply and refuse disposal, among other things. In every locality, Medical Officers of Health and Sanitary Inspectors were to be appointed, under the central control of the Local Government Board. By the turn of the century, British towns were much healthier, although still far below present-day standards. The average expectation of life increased by ten years between 1850 and 1900—a measure of the rapid progress in public health. By this time, most of the basic sanitary services were established and the public health problem had become largely a housing problem.

The demand for houses was greater than the supply right through the nineteenth century. The enormous increase in population caused severe overcrowding, especially in the growing industrial towns. According to the 1891 census, over

10 per cent of the people lived more than two to a room. Yet not until 1868 was any attempt made to give town councils power to deal with housing. Even then very little was achieved, for the authorities were reluctant to interfere with private property. (Sanitary improvements did not meet this obstacle because they did not threaten a landlord's property—on the contrary they increased its value.)

As a young man, Benjamin Disraeli had urged the state to use its powers to protect industrial workers. Some thirty years later, he tried to turn words into actions. In 1875 his Government passed an Artisans' Dwellings Act which gave councils powers to take over and clear whole slum areas. Although it was not compulsory, some councils acted promptly. In London, nearly 30,000 were rehoused in the next thirty years, and in Birmingham, under its reforming mayor, Joseph Chamberlain, over 16 hectares of slum land were purchased for £1,500,000 and cleared.

Unfortunately many of the cleared sites became, in the words of one observer, 'a cemetery for cats and a last resting place for worn-out boots and kettles' before private builders could be found to redevelop the land. Local authorities were

Blue Gate Fields—a London slum in the 1870s

not urged to build houses themselves until 1890. Even then, little was done until after the 1914–18 war. It was all very well to knock down slums, but replacing them with better houses, at rents within the reach of poorer families, was not so easy.

Central and Local Government

Up to 1867, only about one man in ten could vote in parliamentary elections (no women had the vote until 1919). The right to vote was based on property and wealth, so the upper and middle classes had almost a monopoly of political power. However, when the state took on responsibility for improving the living conditions of working people, it seemed common sense to give them a share in deciding who should rule. In 1867, therefore, a Parliamentary Reform Act almost doubled the electorate and redistributed the seats in the House of Commons in favour of the expanding towns. All male householders in the boroughs could now vote. A further Act of 1884 put agricultural labourers on the same footing as town workers by giving the vote to householders in the counties.

In addition, the corrupt system of open voting was replaced by secret ballot in 1872. There was now no need for a man to declare his political views in public and risk offending those in authority over him. Reform of the electoral system was accompanied by a quickening in the pace of social reform. Ordinary working men formed the majority of the electorate after 1884, and could therefore bring pressure to bear on the policies of the political parties.

In step with these developments, the system of local government was also reshaped. No social reform could be effective without well-organised local authorities to carry out the day-to-day administration. Borough councils, elected by the ratepayers, had been active in the industrial towns since the 1830s. Birmingham, under Joseph Chamberlain, showed how effective the best of them could be. As Chamberlain said, Birmingham 'was parked, paved, assized, marketed, gas and watered and improved—all as a result of three years active work'.

Progress was slower in the countryside. Even in the 1880s

country dwellers had little say in the running of their locality. An important Local Government Act (1888) remedied this by setting up elected county councils. Some sixty large towns were made separate county boroughs, with the same powers as county councils. A further Act of 1894 established nearly 7,000 parish councils and also the system of urban and rural district councils, all based on direct election by the residents. The strengthening of local government was a necessary first step before any kind of Welfare State, as we know it, could be established.

As the Victorian Age drew to a close, the people could look back on over half a century of social reform. Parliament had helped to secure improvements in the mines, factories and workshops. The vote had been extended to every male house-holder. Public sanitary services were well established and a start had been made on the task of slum clearance. Though the worker's lot was still harsh by modern standards, it was much better than it had ever been. It was in these reforms that the state's broader concern with the problems of living in an industrial society had its first cautious origins.

Joseph Chamberlain—mayor of Birmingham and social reformer

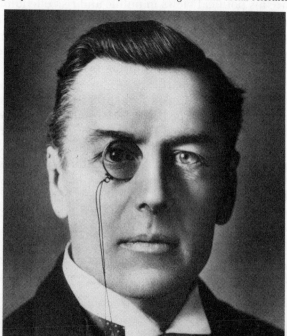

3 'Board School Brats'

No matter how much working conditions and living standards were improved, the labouring classes could never develop into full and equal members of society without education. Until the late nineteenth century, however, schooling was a private matter, left for parents to decide. The well-to-do could afford the necessary school fees, but many working-class children were deprived of education because their parents were unable to pay for it. Even when free elementary schools were provided by private charity, many parents preferred to keep their children at work to help make up the family income.

Voluntary Schools

Early in the nineteenth century, various private and charity schools were established to cater for working-class children. Well-meaning ladies sometimes held small classes in their homes, charging a few pennies a week. The instruction in these 'dame schools' was usually dull and mechanical, and often worthless. In the absence of government regulations, there was nothing to stop people from opening schools in their own homes, even though they might be extremely ignorant. Thomas Wood, son of a Yorkshire weaver, wrote this about his education by an old man in the 1820s: 'I only remember one book . . . a big Bible. The little ones learnt letters out of it. Bigger ones learnt to read. I am not quite sure we ever read anything but the first chapter of St John . . . My school life came to an end when I was about eight years old.'

Many people thought the poor needed instruction in religion, which meant reading the Bible. Church societies therefore began to run free elementary schools in some areas. There was great rivalry between the Nonconformist 'British and

'The monitorial system'—older boys teach the younger ones in groups

Foreign Schools Society' (1808) and the Church of England 'National Society for the Education of the Poor' (1811). Both were short of money and teachers, so they operated a 'monitorial system'. One master taught a select group of older pupils, the monitors, and these, in turn, taught the juniors. One of the founders of this system, Andrew Bell, said: 'Give me twenty-four pupils today, and I will give you twenty-four teachers tomorrow.' It was possible for one master to supervise the teaching of hundreds of pupils by this method—but there was no guarantee that they learned anything.

In addition, there were some factory schools, Sunday schools and, later, workhouse schools. None of these aimed to teach more than 'habits of industry and piety' to children of the poor. Pupils were fitted for the place in society to which they had been born, and taught to obey their social superiors. Despite these developments, a majority of children were receiving no education at all when Queen Victoria came to the throne (1837). The first sign of government interest was a grant of £20,000 to the church societies in 1833 for school building. The grant was increased to £30,000 in 1839 and a special Education Committee set up. Even then, the government was spending more in a year on the Queen's stables than on the education of the poor.

The Secretary of the Education Committee, James Kay Shuttleworth, thought lack of education was an important cause of poverty and ill health. He said the poor were too ignorant to look after themselves properly, and the government should take more responsibility for providing schools. Kay Shuttleworth was not satisfied with the 'monitorial system', so he made great efforts to increase the supply of trained teachers. He started a teachers' training college at Battersea, and, from this example, voluntary colleges sprang up in other areas. To get over the immediate teacher shortage, Kay Shuttleworth began a 'pupil teacher' system, which he had seen working successfully in Holland. Pupil teachers were like apprentices. During the day they helped the older teachers, and in their spare time they studied themselves and took lessons, usually from the headmaster. After five years they took exams to become assistant teachers or qualify for a place at a training college.

Education for the poor still involved little more than elementary religious knowledge and the bare essentials of reading and writing. Anything further was regarded as extravagance, although Kay Shuttleworth thought the working classes needed more, to enrich their drab lives. He appointed more inspectors (there were only two in 1839) and expanded teachers' training facilities. By the middle of the century, state grants had risen to £500,000 a year. The middle classes were now more prepared to accept the idea of government aid for elementary education. There was a growing need in industry for people who could read and write. Also, it was widely believed that crime, unrest and drunkenness in the towns were direct results of ignorance, and that uneducated workers might be a danger to the peace and security of the nation.

Meanwhile the voluntary schools went on expanding, through the efforts of generous and far-sighted individuals. One of these we have already met as a factory reformer—Lord Ashley. By about 1850, with the ten-and-a-half-hour day achieved, Ashley began to take an interest in the Ragged Schools Union, which had been set up to provide free education for children of poor parents. Ashley soon became President, and set about building new schools and improving old

A ragged school in 1846

ones. He raised funds to provide food and clothing as well as schooling for those in dire need, and even resorted to begging money from M.P.s as they entered Parliament, to help finance his schemes. He put so much of his own money into charitable work that he was often penniless, but this did not trouble him. He once said: 'I would rather be President of the Ragged Schools Union than have the command of armies or wield the destiny of empires.'

For all their efforts, however, the voluntary schools could not cope alone with the increasing demand for education. The state would have to do more. Reformers had long suggested that schools should be financed out of the local rates, but the government was slow to act because of the difficulties involved. The well-off were reluctant to tax themselves in order to pay for the education of their social inferiors, and the Churches had been squabbling among themselves for thirty years about how the available money should be spent. Rate-payers who belonged to the Church of England objected to paying for schools which did not teach their religion, while Nonconformists took a similar view when they were asked to give aid to Church of England schools.

'Payment by Results'

In 1861 a Royal Commission on Education suggested a system of paying grants to schools 'out of the county rates, in consideration of the attainment of a certain degree of knowledge by the children in the school during the year preceding the payment'. Robert Lowe, Vice-President of the Department of Education, liked this idea. It promised something definite in return for money spent. As he put it: 'If it is not cheap, it shall be efficient; if it is not efficient, it shall be cheap.' In the following year, therefore, his Revised Code established a system of 'payment by results'.

Inspectors visited grant-aided schools each year to examine children in the 'three Rs' (reading, 'riting and 'rithmetic) and up to twelve shillings (60p) per child was paid, depending on the result of the examination. Teachers, realising the importance of the occasion, often resorted to underhand methods such as signalling the answers to the children from behind the inspector's back. 'Payment by results' certainly helped to even out standards from one district to another, and in some cases made the teachers more efficient, but it was a bad system in other ways. For instance bright children were neglected while the teacher concentrated on bringing the slower ones up to the required standard.

By this time, just under half of the 3½ million children in England and Wales were going regularly to school. Apart from the religious disagreements, further progress was hampered by doubts about whether schools should be paid for out of the rates. Another Royal Commission (1868) put both sides of the argument. On the one hand, 'it is a matter of national interest that intellectual ability, in whatever rank it may be found, should have the fullest opportunities of cultivation'. But, against this view, 'it seems more likely that people will learn the value of education by being perpetually urged to make the sacrifices necessary to procure it for their children, than by being set free from all care or labour for the purpose'.

The thing which really tipped the scales was the 1867 Parliamentary Reform Act, which gave the vote to working-class householders in the boroughs. Robert Lowe said, 'We must educate our future masters'. By this he meant that the new voters should at least be able to read and write before they chose their Member of Parliament. Another factor was the advances in education being made in countries such as Germany and the United States, which had become Britain's main trading rivals. Britain's industrial supremacy was sure to be lost if half her children remained uneducated. It was time for decisive government action.

Board Schools

An Education Act of 1870 was the turning point. Parliament ordered the election of local School Boards in all districts where proper schools were not already provided by the religious societies. These Boards could provide elementary schools for the five-to-ten age group, paid for out of the local rates. Parents were to be excused fees if they were very poor, although attendance was not compulsory. The Boards were to assist in the maintenance of Church schools but not in the building of them, which went on, as before, with the aid of direct government grants. Most of the Board Schools were drab and badly equipped, and classes of eighty or ninety were common, but at least it was the start of some sort of 'system'.

Sherlock Holmes, in one of Conan Doyle's famous detective stories, said of the Board Schools: 'Lighthouses, my boy! Beacons of the future! Capsules, with hundreds of bright little seeds in each, out of which will spring the wiser, better England of the future.' He was correct in his prediction, although at the time most of the pupils were far from being 'bright little seeds'. They were mostly dirty and ragged, with skin diseases and running noses and ears. More fortunate middle-class children, from expensive private schools, called them 'Board School brats'. Before the 'brats' could be educated, they had to be civilised. Schooling encouraged habits of punctuality, discipline and cleanliness which, in time, increased their self-respect and made them less hostile to 'book learning'.

By 1880 there were enough schools to make possible compulsory attendance up to the age of ten (gradually raised to twelve by the end of the century). Many parents objected to this, saying they could not afford to lose the wages of their children, if they had started work. To make compulsory

Boys of the same age in a school in Bermondsey, London, in 1894 (above) and 1924 (below)

attendance possible, many Boards had to arrange for cheap school meals and medical attention, along with the distribution of charity clothing for the most ragged ones. Fees were low, but many families still had great difficulty in finding the money. Even twopence (1p) a week was a lot of money when the difference between weekly earnings and the rent was often only two or three shillings (10–15p). Therefore elementary education was made free in 1891.

The Beginnings of State Secondary Education

So far we have only considered elementary, or primary, education. Until the end of the nineteenth century there was no thought of providing a national system of secondary education for the poor. Secondary education was restricted to those who could afford the fees of private, grammar or public schools. But clever children from Board Schools needed more than just elementary education. By the 1890s, some Boards provided 'higher grade schools', and county councils were allowed to support technical, evening and other advanced classes. However, these opportunities were open to only a small proportion of the working classes.

An arithmetic class, 1891

By the Education Act of 1902, Parliament made secondary schools the concern of the state. The Boards were abolished and their duties taken over by county and county borough councils. They had done well, providing nearly $2\frac{1}{2}$ million school places, but most Boards were too small to be really efficient. The new Local Education Authorities could now create their own secondary schools, charging fees. However, from 1907, some free scholarship places were left open to the cleverest children from the elementary schools. Government grants helped to take some of the financial burden off the local rates.

So free secondary education was now available for those who could show themselves worthy of it. There were very few free places at first. Even by 1914 less than one in twenty from the elementary schools won a scholarship to secondary school. Nevertheless education for the poor had come a long way since the days of the monitorial system. An 'educational ladder' had been built which could be climbed by able and hardworking children from any social background.

4 Poverty in York, 1899

Before we leave the Victorian Age, two important questions need to be asked. First, how far had the nineteenth-century reforms improved the living standards of working-class people? Second, what further improvements were most urgently required? We can get some way towards the answers by trying to find out how much poverty existed in Britain at the turn of the century, and the reasons for it.

Seebohm Rowntree

To make the picture more sharply defined we shall focus on just one city, York, through the eyes of Seebohm Rowntree, who made a special study of its working classes in 1899. Seebohm, as you may have guessed, was the son of a cocoa and chocolate manufacturer. He began work as a chemist in the family business in 1889, at the age of eighteen. In the same year, a book was published which was to make a great impression on him. It was the first of a seventeen-volume survey by Charles Booth, a Liverpool shipowner, on *The Life and Labour of the People of London*. Booth discovered that about a third of London's population lived in deep poverty, earning about £1 a week or less.

Seebohm soon became greatly concerned with the problems of working-class life, especially the extent and causes of poverty. He decided to conduct a survey of his own to compare conditions in a smaller town with those found in London by Booth. As he put it: 'One knows there is a great deal of poverty in the East End of London but I wonder whether there is in provincial cities. Why not investigate York?' Certainly if Rowntree could show that a great deal of poverty existed in a city like York, it would make the public and politicians

The Shambles, York, pictured at the turn of the century

take notice and prove wrong many of Booth's critics who claimed London was exceptional.

Early in 1899, with the aid of an interviewer and a secretary, Rowntree began a house-to-house inquiry, covering the whole working-class population of York. This involved 46,754 people, two-thirds of the total population. The keeping of servants was taken as the decisive factor in distinguishing between the working classes and those of a higher social rank.

The Extent of Poverty

Rowntree found 20,302 people living in a state of poverty. In other words, almost 28 per cent of the whole population of York did not have enough food, fuel and clothing to keep them in good health. Undoubtedly the Victorian reformers had left many problems unsolved. Of those in poverty, about a third did not have enough money coming in each week to live a normal, healthy life *even if they spent every penny wisely*. Victorian 'remedies' like thrift were of no use to these people. They could not be expected to save money when they did not have

29

Elegance and squalor—York Minster surrounded by crowded slums

enough for essentials. The remaining two-thirds had enough income to give them the bare necessities, but they spent some portion of it unwisely. Consequently they were forced to go short on food or clothing, or both.

These figures were very close to those arrived at by Charles Booth. He had found just over 30 per cent in poverty in East London, working on roughly the same definition of poverty as Rowntree. So it seemed likely that almost a third of Britain's town dwellers were forced to go without some of the necessities of a civilised life. Such conditions were not confined to the towns. A few years later, Rowntree discovered that agricultural labourers were even worse off.

What was it like living in poverty? Rowntree found that most families in this situation could afford nothing better than a damp, dark slum. Often one water tap supplied several houses and, in many cases, this was fixed to the wall of the lavatory. 'Midden privvies' were the general rule in the slums. In these the functions of lavatory and dustbin were combined in a brick-lined pit, which was often shared by several families. Rowntree said: 'A large number of them are found inches

30

deep in liquid filth, or so full of refuse as to reach above the cemented portions of the walls.'

Broken window panes were stuffed with rags or pasted over with brown paper and the smell from the overcrowded slums could be almost unbearable. This is a typical example of living conditions taken from a Sanitary Inspector's notebook: '2 rooms. In the lower one a brick floor is in holes. Fireplace without grate in bottom. Wooden floor of upper room has large holes admitting numbers of mice. Roof very defective, rain falling through on to the bed in wet weather.' In these conditions it was not surprising that one child out of every four born died before it was a year old and many of those who lived were stunted and deformed. As Rowntree put it: 'It is Nature's universal law that all living things tend to adapt themselves to their environment'. Public Health and Housing Acts still left much to be desired. There was not even a full-time Medical Officer of Health in York until 1900.

The diet of the poverty-stricken slum dwellers was often seriously deficient. Many families could not afford butcher's meat at all. Rowntree asked some housewives to keep accounts of the money they spent and the menus provided. Here is a typical example of the diet of a poor family:

	BREAKFAST	LUNCH/ DINNER	TEA	SUPPER
SATURDAY	Bread, butter, boiled egg, coffee	Meat, potatoes, pie, tea	Bread, butter, tea	Roast potatoes, tea
SUNDAY	Bread, butter, coffee	Beef, potatoes, pudding, tea	Bread, butter, tea	Meat, bread, tea
MONDAY	Bread, butter, coffee	Meat, potatoes, bread, tea	Bread, butter, tea	
TUESDAY	Bread, butter, tea	Hash, bread, tea	Bread, butter, tea	
WEDNESDAY	Bread, butter, coffee	Liver, potatoes, onions, tea	Bread, butter, tea, dripping	
THURSDAY	Bread, butter, coffee	Bread, dripping, tea	Bread, dripping, tea	
FRIDAY	Bread, butter, tea	Bread, butter, toast tea	Toast, butter, tea	

This meagre diet accounted for almost half the family's total income; the rest went mainly on fuel and rent. Although it may have contained enough bulk to fight off the feeling of hunger, it did not give sufficient nourishment to keep the family in good health. Notice how it tails off towards the end of the week. From looking at the family menu you can work out the day on which the father was paid. Extras like clothing often had to be paid for by going short of food. One woman said: 'If there's anything extra to buy, such as a pair of boots for one of the children, me and the children goes without dinner.'

Many families above the 'poverty line' at the time of the survey had earlier been in poverty when their children were too young to work. At a time when children's wages made such an important contribution to the family's living standards it is easy to see why there were so many objections to compulsory education. Children were taken away from school at the earliest possible moment. One boy in a Board School asked his teacher:

'"Please, sir, what time is it?"

"Half-past ten, my lad, but what's the matter?"

"Please, sir, then may I go, sir? My mother said I should be fourteen at ten-thirty this morning, and I could leave school when I was fourteen, sir."'

Hundreds of people, especially old folk, were only kept out of the workhouse by private charity or assistance from relatives. Some families went short themselves in order to offer poor relations a home. Even so, York's workhouse had about 450 inhabitants; and a further 1,000 received poor relief in their homes. The 'able-bodied' in the workhouse mainly chopped and bundled wood for sale in the city. The children went to elementary school when they were old enough, but for the rest of the time they mixed with the adults—often learning bad habits from them.

The Causes of Poverty

Taking those whose basic incomes were insufficient, Rowntree found two main reasons for their plight. In a quarter of these cases, the chief wage-earner of the family was out of action or dead. He might be ill or disabled, too old to work or unemployed. However, in over half the families in this category the breadwinner was in regular work. His wages were simply too low to meet his family's needs. Unskilled labourers earned on average just under £1 a week in York at this time, yet Rowntree estimated that at least 21s. 8d. (£1.08) was needed to keep a family with three children out of poverty. The belief that a man could always provide for his family if he was thrifty and willing to work hard was shown to be false. However hard he tried, he could not avoid poverty if his earnings were insufficient.

In the case of those whose incomes were sufficient but who failed to spend every penny wisely, it was more difficult to give precise reasons for their poverty. Drink and gambling— in that order—were almost certainly the main causes. When father drank, the children often went supperless to bed. Rowntree deplored these vices, but suggested that men often took to drink and gambling not from weakness of character but because of the appalling conditions under which they lived. Extravagant housekeeping was another cause of poverty. Housewives often spent unwisely through ignorance of what was the best value for money.

Judging from conditions in York, it appeared that the Victorian reforms had not removed the root causes of poverty. The most urgent problem was low wages, but no government wanted to interfere with the right of an employer to pay his workers what he thought fit. Workers would have to fight their own battles through their trade unions. Nevertheless many reformers, including Rowntree, thought there should be national minimum rates of pay to be fixed by Parliament.

Rowntree's findings led many people to look beyond mere *public* health to *personal* health and welfare services. The lives of the poor were precarious. They needed insurance and pensions to give them a regular income when they were not earning. Better-off workers could afford to contribute to insurance schemes run by trade unions and Friendly Societies, but few unskilled workers could spare the money for subscriptions to such schemes. The state would have to help these people. The challenge for the twentieth century was clear.

5 Foundation Stones

In the early years of the twentieth century, before the Great
War of 1914–18, Parliament began to turn its attention from
empire-building overseas to the problem of poverty on its own
doorstep. This policy had been recommended back in 1890
by 'General' William Booth, founder of the Salvation Army.
In his book, *Darkest England*, he suggested that the 'white
man's burden' of 'civilising' Africans and other poor peoples
of the world should begin at home, where wretched slum
dwellers were forced to live like savages.

In 1902, an American writer, Jack London, lived for a time
among the poor of the East End of London. He found that
most wages were too low for people to live decently. Thousands walked the streets, day and night, without proper food
and shelter, because of a general shortage of both work and
housing. He warned the British that their country would suffer a serious decline if workers continued to live in these conditions: 'Brutalised, degraded and dull, . . . It is absurd to
think for an instant that they can compete with the workers
of the New World.' The rot had already set in. Nearly half
the volunteers for the army during the Boer War (1899–1902)
were rejected because of ill health. In London, one adult
worker in every three died on public charity—in a workhouse,
hospital or asylum.

'The Liberal Landslide'

The well-to-do, secure in their world of plenty, were still not
disturbed. They said poverty would die out of its own accord
as Britain got richer. However, this attitude was rejected by
the Liberal Party in Parliament. Out of office since 1895, they
were determined to make war on poverty once they got back

David Lloyd George—'father of the Welfare State'

to power. In the general election of 1905, working-class voters put their faith in the Liberals, helping them to gain a massive majority. The way was now clear for them to carry out their policy of reform.

There were many able men in the new ministry, not least among them David Lloyd George and Winston Churchill. Lloyd George, often called 'the father of the Welfare State', had greater insight into the real needs of working people than any Cabinet Minister before him. 'In so far as poverty is due to circumstances over which man has no control,' he said, 'then the state should step in to the very utmost limit of its resources.' When Lloyd George became Chancellor of the Exchequer in 1908, Winston Churchill took over from him as President of the Board of Trade, at the age of thirty-three. There was no doubt where his sympathies lay. 'The cause of Liberalism is the cause of the left-out millions', he said.

35

Child Welfare

In the next few years, the Liberals laid the foundations for the Welfare State. The needs of children were their first priority, for the best way of improving the condition of the people was to start with the rising generation. Clean water and better sanitation were not enough; babies needed good food and pure milk if they were to escape disease, and mothers required guidance. A number of local authorities had recently opened clean milk depots and appointed health visitors to advise parents on infant care. After 1906, with government assistance, infant welfare clinics were opened in many areas. The value of these improvements can be seen in the following figures:

INFANT MORTALITY RATE
(deaths of infants under one year old per 1,000 live births)

1901	151
1905	128
1912	95

It is now about twelve per thousand, which shows how much room for improvement still remained after 1912.

Older children had been partly the responsibility of the whole community ever since Parliament compelled them to go to school. Compulsory education itself highlighted the evils of poverty. Hordes of ragged, diseased and starving children now came into the public eye, instead of hiding away in dingy slums where their plight was ignored. Consequently in many towns charity organisations provided meals for children who were too hungry to learn, and clothing for the most ragged ones.

The Liberals set out to provide school meals in all areas. By an Act of 1906, Local Education Authorities could either make use of existing voluntary schemes or, where these were absent, provide meals themselves. Only children who were 'unable by reason of lack of food to take full advantage of the education provided for them' received meals, but it was still an important step forward. 'I'm not used to having a Sunday dinner every day' was a common remark from children in the early days of the scheme. By 1914, over 150,000 children were receiving school meals—on Saturdays and during the holidays as well as in term-time.

Undernourishment was only part of a general health problem among children. A Royal Commission (1909) reported that:

'Nearly the whole of the children of a slum quarter may go on year after year suffering from adenoids, inflamed glands, enlarged tonsils, defects of eyesight, chronic ear discharges . . . which will eventually prevent many of them from earning their livelihood.'

From 1907, local authorities were compelled to have children in elementary schools medically examined. As a result, many appalling facts came to light. In Liverpool, for example, over 80 per cent of the girls examined were infested with bugs, fleas and lice. Parents were made responsible for obtaining the necessary treatment for their children, but many neglected their duty. Therefore the Board of Education gave grants, after 1912, to make more treatment possible.

The Government's concern for the welfare of children extended beyond their schooldays. Juvenile Employment Bureaux were started in 1910 to help school-leavers find suitable jobs. These were only part of a whole new structure of services catering for the special needs of the young. Borstals and Probation Courts were introduced by the Liberals (1909) in the hope of preventing young offenders from hardening into criminals. Imprisonment of children was abolished. The emphasis was now on prevention rather than punishment. The new attitude to the young even extended to making it an offence to allow children to beg, or buy cigarettes.

A child being medically inspected, 1912

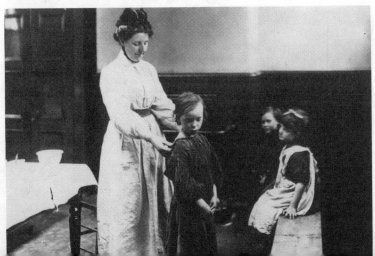

Old Age Pensions and 'The People's Budget'

The idea of a state pensions scheme had been discussed in Britain ever since Germany introduced one in 1889. Bismarck, the German Chancellor at that time, said it was unfair to give soldiers pensions whilst allowing 'the veterans of industry to die in misery'. When the Liberals came to power they promised old age pensions as soon as they could spare the money. By 1908, a way was found to finance a state scheme which, in the words of the new Prime Minister, Herbert Asquith, had been 'long deserved and long deferred'. Pensions were granted to the over-seventies, provided they were British subjects and their income was not above twelve shillings (60p) a week. The pension varied between one and five shillings (5–25p) weekly, depending on the pensioner's income. Payments were made at post offices.

Pensions were the first truly nationwide social service. The Government admitted that the weekly payments were small but said they could not afford more. 'We have not pretended to carry the toiler on to dry land,' said Churchill. 'What we have done is to strap a lifebelt around him.' Even so, he pointed out that: 'Nearly eight millions of money are being sent circulating through unusual channels, long frozen by poverty; circulating in the homes of the poor, flowing through the little shops that cater to their needs.' Old people were

Winston Churchill speaking in public

delighted to have this regular income. They were now less dependent on the goodwill of relations or the grudging help of the poor law. As Lloyd George said: 'We are lifting the shadow of the workhouse from the homes of the poor.'

To pay for social welfare schemes, especially pensions, Lloyd George estimated that an extra £16 million would have to be raised in taxes. Introducing his budget of 1909, he said: 'This is a war budget. It is for raising money to wage implacable warfare on poverty and squalidness.' As well as increased taxes on drink and tobacco, and a new car licence, Lloyd George raised the income tax. It was scaled, so that the rich paid 1*s*. 2*d*.(6p) in the pound while those with incomes below £3,000 a year paid 9*d*.(4p). A further 'super tax' of 6*d*.(2½p) in the pound was levied on the rich. In addition, Lloyd George placed a series of heavy taxes on profits gained from property—mainly rents and sales of land.

Punch cartoon showing Lloyd George as he must have appeared to the wealthy ruling class (plutocrats) after his budget

RICH FARE.

The Giant Lloyd-Gog-nevier: "FEE, FI, FO, FAT,
I SMELL THE BLOOD OF A PLUTOCRAT;
BE HE ALIVE OR BE HE DEAD,
I'LL GRIND HIS BONES TO MAKE MY BREAD."

The 'People's Budget', as it was called, raised a storm of opposition from the wealthy classes. Income tax increases were bad enough, but property taxes were more than they would stand for. The Conservatives, many of them landowners, used their majority in the House of Lords to reject the budget. This infuriated the Liberals. After a long struggle, the Government forced the Lords to accept the budget. Soon afterwards, the Parliament Act (1911) drastically reduced the powers of the House of Lords for the future. The scene was set for further increases in government spending on the welfare of the needy.

Unemployment and Labour Exchanges

There had been signs of a new approach to the problem of unemployment in the previous Conservative ministry. In 1897 Parliament made it compulsory for some employers to pay compensation to injured workers. The Liberals extended Workmen's Compensation (1906) to include all injuries at work and even some industrial diseases. Another Conservative measure, the Unemployed Workmen Act (1905), attempted for the first time to deal with unemployment on a nationwide scale. Local authorities could form Distress Committees in each borough. Work was provided, where possible, and in suitable cases emigration overseas was arranged. The Liberals renewed the Act, granting £200,000 from the Treasury to increase local funds. From now on, unemployment was seen as a national responsibility.

A new labour exchange, 1910

William Beveridge, a young civil servant, had made a close study of unemployment. He was greatly impressed by German 'labour exchanges', where both employers and workers registered their requirements. By this means, the unemployed could be made aware of job vacancies. The idea was not entirely new in Britain, but Beveridge's plan was more ambitious than anything attempted before. He soon converted Churchill to the idea, and, early in 1910, the first eighty-three labour exchanges opened. They were part of a wider scheme, based on insurance, which was soon to be operated through them.

Unemployment Insurance

The climax of social reform in this period was the National Insurance Act of 1911. It was in two parts, the second dealing with unemployment. 'Through insurance', said Churchill, 'families can be secured against catastrophes which otherwise would smash them up for ever.' As we have seen, many workers did insure themselves, through private organisations like Friendly Societies. But poorly paid workers could not afford to pay subscriptions high enough to give them adequate benefits. In any case, whether they could afford it or not, many preferred to 'take a chance' rather than pay for something they might never need. The Liberals hoped to bring insurance within the reach of those who needed it most by offering a state scheme, with higher benefits for lower contributions.

Because state insurance was a new departure—'a risky adventure into the unknown', Beveridge later called it—the 1911 scheme began on a small scale. Unemployment insurance was restricted to a few 'precarious' trades—building, shipbuilding, mechanical engineering, ironfounding, vehicle construction and sawmilling. If successful, the scheme was to be extended to other trades in the future. Workers over sixteen, their employers and the state each contributed $2\frac{1}{2}d$ (1p) a week, so spreading the cost over the whole community. In return, 7s. (35p) a week was payable at a labour exchange from the second week of unemployment. This benefit continued for a maximum of fifteen weeks in any one year, provided enough contributions had been paid beforehand.

41

William Beveridge here describes some further details of the scheme:

'We adopted the German plan of raising contributions from employers and employees by stamps attached to cards; but we should almost certainly have been forced to think of that ourselves. . . . In so far as we used any working models we used the trade unions— in particular their practice of requiring signature of a vacant book in working hours as proof of unemployment, and their common provision of a waiting period before benefit began.'

Benefits were not enough to provide a living on their own and, in any case, there was a time limit on them. So workers were not encouraged to remain idle—they still needed to find a job as soon as possible. Taken all round, the scheme was a great success. Unlike poor relief, workers paid part of the cost of unemployment insurance themselves. Consequently they did not have the feeling of 'living on charity' when they were out of work.

Health Insurance

Part I of the 1911 Act introduced another long-awaited scheme 'to provide for insurance against loss of health and for prevention and cure of sickness'. Again, Germany provided the model. There had been a marked improvement in the condition of the German people as a result of health insurance, at very small cost to the state. As in the case of unemployment, Friendly Society and trade union health insurance schemes had long been available in Britain to those who could afford the subscriptions. But only about half the working population was covered in this way against sickness, and, even then, 250,000 policies lapsed every year because members failed to keep up regular payments. The uninsured had to get medical treatment under the poor law. This varied from adequate care in some of the newer infirmaries to grudging reception into an old-fashioned mixed workhouse.

'The community must lend its powerful aid,' said Lloyd George. However, there were problems to be overcome first— especially the opposition of doctors to the plan. They were mostly in favour of a state medical service, but thought they should run it themselves. The Government, on the other hand, wished to operate through the Friendly Societies, creating so-called 'approved societies'. After much argument, which threatened to wreck the whole plan, a compromise was reached which gave doctors better conditions than they had ever had before.

All wage-earners between sixteen and seventy had to belong to the scheme if they earned less than £3 a week. Their weekly contribution was 4*d.* (just over 1½p), to which their employers and the state added a further 5*d.* (2p) between them. Payments were recorded by means of stamps stuck on individual cards. In return, free medical attention, with medicine, was given. This did not include hospital or specialist services, however, just 'simple doctoring'. When work was lost through sickness, 10*s.* (50p) a week was paid by the approved society, from the fourth day of the illness. This lasted for a maximum of twenty-six weeks, after which 'disablement benefit' (half the full amount) could be claimed. An additional 30*s.* (£1.50) 'maternity benefit' was paid on the birth of each child.

Most workers were delighted at being given 'ninepence worth of insurance for fourpence', but there was still some

Leaflet explaining the new scheme of National Insurance against sickness, issued by the Government, 1911

opposition. Domestic servants claimed they were looked after and paid while they were sick without having to bother about insurance. Lloyd George replied that not everyone had generous employers and it was therefore desirable for the whole community to co-operate in order to benefit those in the greatest need. Ladies who employed servants said it was beneath their dignity to 'lick their stamps'. However this hardship received little sympathy.

Churchill summed up the importance of both parts of the 1911 Act: 'National Insurance . . . is the most decisive step yet taken upon the path of social organisation. . . . The cruel waste of disease and unemployment, breaking down men and women, breaking up homes and families, will for the first time be encountered by the whole strength of the nation.'

Minimum Wages

The demands of Seebohm Rowntree and others for a national minimum wage presented a great problem for the Government. Since low wages were probably the greatest single cause of poverty, it was likely that a legal minimum wage would do more than anything else to relieve misery. Nevertheless, the Liberals were certain to be called dictators if they tried to interfere in such matters. They felt they must, as a general rule, leave wages to be settled between employers and trade unions.

However the Liberal Government made two exceptions to the rule. The first concerned miners, whose dangerous work for low wages gained them great public sympathy. Parliament, having reduced their working day to eight hours (1908), created a minimum wage board for miners in 1912. The second exception involved the so-called 'sweated' trades—for example, tailoring and lace, chain and paper-box making. These workers, crammed into tiny 'sweat shops', which were often little more than attics, were the lowest paid of all. They were not organised into trade unions, so they had no effective method of bargaining for higher wages. To meet this need, Trade Boards were set up by the Government, from 1909, to fix minimum wages in the 'sweated' industries.

Churchill once defined the Liberal policy as 'drawing a line, below which we will not allow persons to live and labour'. Although the Government was reluctant to impose a general minimum wage, its other policies went a long way towards achieving a minimum standard of living. By 1914 working people could look forward to a state pension in old age, and some of the dread of unemployment and sickness was removed by the knowledge that money would still be coming in. These reforms struck for the first time at the root causes of poverty. Instead of merely providing workhouses for the very worst cases, the Liberals had begun to develop more specialised services to meet particular needs.

Poster advertising National Health Insurance. The 'doctor' is Lloyd George

THE DAWN OF HOPE.

Mr. LLOYD GEORGE'S National Health Insurance Bill provides for the insurance of the Worker in case of Sickness.

Support the Liberal Government
in their policy of
SOCIAL REFORM.

6 The Shadow of Unemployment

The Great War of 1914–18 brought the period of Liberal reform to an end. Nevertheless, after Britain's 'bloodstained stagger to victory', as Lloyd George called it, the returning soldiers and their families looked forward to the future with high hopes. Lloyd George, Prime Minister since 1916, promised 'a land fit for heroes', with government spending being diverted from the demands of war to an attack on poverty. The first signs were encouraging. Even before the peace treaty was signed, the vote was extended to all men over twenty-one and given to women for the first time—although they had to be over thirty and either ratepayers or the wives of ratepayers. A general election was held almost immediately, and the wartime Coalition Government was returned to power with an enormous majority.

Unemployment Insurance Extended

Plans were soon made to expand the existing social services, starting with National Insurance against unemployment. The original scheme of 1911 had covered only a few 'precarious' industries. Although the number of trades was slightly enlarged in 1916, millions of workers were still left out. To remedy this, the Government introduced a much wider scheme in 1920. It covered everybody earning less than £5 a week, except farm labourers and domestic and civil servants. Weekly contributions were much the same as in the 1911 scheme (see page 41), but benefits were increased to 15s. (75p) for men and 12s (60p) for women. These could be claimed for up to fifteen weeks in any year—provided the labour exchange was unable to offer a suitable job. In the following year, allowances for 'dependants' were added: 5s. (25p) for a wife and 1s. (5p) for each child.

The Depression Begins

By 1921 life was practically back to normal. Everywhere people talked of 'business as usual'. Then, suddenly, the numbers of unemployed began to increase alarmingly. By the summer of 1921, two million men were out of work—one in every seven of working age. There was no immediate panic, however, for everyone expected the situation to improve very soon. They were not to know that British foreign trade was entering upon a period of rapid decline. From 1921 to 1940, the numbers of unemployed never fell below a million.

This prolonged period of high unemployment was all the more surprising because, for a short time after the war, British industry had enjoyed a 'boom' (increase of business). Every-

THE MOUNTAINEER.

RATEPAYER (*to the Premier*). "I KNOW YOU'RE ALWAYS KEEN ON MOUNTAINS, SIR. HAVE YOU NOTICED THIS ONE?"

where there had been a great demand for goods which had been scarce during wartime. However, by 1921, when more normal trading conditions returned, it was clear that Britain had lost many of her former overseas markets. Britain's share of world trade had been decreasing slowly for half a century, but there had never before been such a dramatic decline in so short a period. Many foreign customers, forced to find other sources of supply during the war, found they could now manage with fewer British goods. Until Britain could find new customers or recover lost markets, there was simply not enough work to go round.

The timing of the trade depression was particularly unfortunate because the new system of unemployment insurance had already been worked out. It was based on the expectation of no more than 4 per cent out of work at any one time. In fact, the unemployment rate never fell below 10 per cent for almost twenty years. So by the time the new scheme came into operation it was already out of date. Hundreds of thousands of workers exhausted their fifteen weeks of benefit without any sign of a job. A further re-shaping of National Insurance was needed if the jobless were to be kept off the poor law. However, throughout the 1920s, governments simply made adjustments to the original plan, hoping the crisis would soon be over. 'Extended benefits'—nicknamed the 'dole'—were introduced as a temporary measure until the worst was over. But the worst was still to come, and extended benefits had themselves to be extended.

Unemployment did not affect the whole country equally. For the majority of people, the 1920s and 1930s was a period of steady improvement in wages and living standards. This was especially true of the areas with new, expanding industries such as building, electrical equipment and motor engineering, mostly in south-eastern England and the Midlands. The minority, who suffered grim unemployment, lived in areas of declining industry, mainly in the north of England, central Scotland and south Wales. Here the main industries were those that had made Britain a great industrial power in the nineteenth century—coal, iron and steel, shipbuilding and textiles. Unfortunately these were the hardest hit when Britain's share of overseas trade fell.

Queue of unemployed outside a labour exchange

Life 'On the Dole'

In the 'depressed areas' the long queue of unemployed outside the labour exchange, waiting to 'sign on', became a regular part of life. In his novel *Love on the Dole* (1933) Walter Greenwood described a typical scene at a labour exchange:

'A dozen or so rows of chairs ... were quickly occupied the instant the men rushed in. Those coming later lounged against the wall.

When one of those seated was called to the counter, his immediate neighbour took his seat. The remainder, with much shuffling of feet and grating of chairs, all moved up a place so that none of the chairs ever were vacant, the queue waiting for them often stretching into the yard. The proceedings had come to be known as "musical chairs".'

Another novelist, George Orwell, toured the depressed areas in 1936 and described them in *The Road to Wigan Pier*. He was particularly struck by the patience and good sense shown by the people:

'. . . they realise that losing your job does not mean that you cease to be a human being. Life is still fairly normal . . . Instead of raging against their destiny, they have made things tolerable by lowering their standards ... You can't get much meat for threepence, but you can get a lot of fish-and-chips. . . . Milk costs threepence a pint and even "mild" beer costs fourpence, but . . . you can wring forty cups of tea out of a quarter-pound packet.'

49

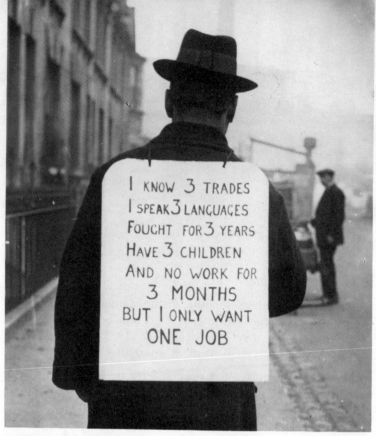

Unemployed man who had not forgotten his sense of humour

There was a time limit on 'extended benefits'. When they finished, the only thing left was the poor law. Because of the large numbers of unemployed in the depressed areas, the Guardians (see p. 7) paid 'outdoor relief'—money which could be claimed without having to enter the workhouse. But because poor relief was financed out of the local rates, the ratepayers in the areas of high unemployment were very hard hit. There were over 600 Poor Law Unions in Britain, yet the main burden of the long-term unemployed fell on fewer than forty of them. The fairest solution to this problem was to take the long-term unemployed off the poor law altogether and make them the responsibility of the nation as a whole through national taxation. This was done, in stages, up to 1934, by which time relief of the unemployed had been taken out of local hands.

The Depression gets Worse—the 'Means Test'

A worldwide financial crisis, beginning with the collapse of the American stock market in 1929, led to a further increase in unemployment. The Prime Minister, James Ramsay MacDonald, was so concerned about the country's financial position that he formed an all-party National Government in 1931. He split with Labour, his former party, in the process. The National Government's policy for recovery was to keep government spending to a minimum. The Labour Party disagreed, saying that the Government should do the reverse and borrow money to invest in public works like roads, houses and schools to create jobs for the unemployed.

The unemployed suffered from the National Government's economy drive. In 1931, benefits for the insured were cut by 10 per cent. The long-term unemployed were now given a 'means test'. This meant that a man claiming extended benefit was turned over to the Public Assistance Committee which demanded details of his family's total income before deciding how much he needed. Even if his son had a paper round or his wife had saved a few pounds in the post office, he had to declare these details and his 'dole' would be adjusted accordingly.

The means test was hated by the unemployed. It was, in Orwell's words, 'an encouragement to the tattle-tale and the informer'. If a child from a Public Assistance home was seen with a new coat or a bicycle, the 'means test man' would soon get to hear about it and call to inquire where it came from. The means test certainly saved the Government several million pounds a year, but the distress it caused was out of all proportion to such savings. Fathers were 'knocked off dole' altogether in some cases because their sons and daughters had regular jobs. Nothing could be more damaging to a man's self-respect than to have to be supported by his children.

Unemployment did not reach its peak until the winter of 1932–33, when almost 3 million people were out of work. Of these, over 500,000 had gone more than a year without a job. In 1934 Parliament passed the twenty-first Unemployment Act within the space of fourteen years. Insurance, based on contributions, was completely separated from assistance ('the

51

dole') and the 10 per cent reduction in benefits, made in 1931, was restored. All the other unemployed, who had exhausted their right to benefits, came under an Unemployment Assistance Board (U.A.B.). The U.A.B., which came into operation in 1936, had offices all over Britain, to relieve the overworked labour exchanges. The amount of assistance paid still depended on a means test, much to the disgust of the unemployed, although the test was made a little less severe.

In addition to cash payments, the U.A.B. was responsible for the welfare of the unemployed. Training centres were established to teach people new skills which would give them more chance of finding work. Help was given to those who wanted to move to areas of the country where there was fuller employment. Older workers, with little chance of finding a job, were often given allotments of land where they grew vegetables and fruit and reared poultry or rabbits for their own families.

Unemployed miner in Wigan—where 17 out of 40 pits were closed, 1939

52

The depressed regions were now called Special Areas. Attempts were made to encourage industries to move to the Special Areas, but they were mostly unsuccessful. Mass unemployment remained for the rest of the 1930s, although it eased a little in some places after about 1934. By this time it had existed for so long that it was accepted as normal. Many young people had reached their mid-twenties without ever having a job. This made it difficult for them to cope with regular employment when it finally came. If you spend years having breakfast at ten or eleven o'clock and sitting around all day, perhaps in a billiard hall or on a park bench, you do not feel much like getting into a routine of disciplined work.

'The Jarrow Crusade'

Some of the unemployed devoted their time to demonstrations and marches, of which the most famous was the 'Jarrow Crusade' of 1936. Situated on the River Tyne, in County Durham, Jarrow had long depended for its livelihood on its shipyard. But in the early 1930s the slump hit Jarrow and the shipyard was dismantled. Quiet descended over the town as the dole queues lengthened. By 1935 three-quarters of the men were out of work. In the following year it was decided to organise a march to London in protest. Throughout the summer funds were collected, a great banner was stitched and boots were repaired. On 5 October, 200 men, chosen from hundreds of volunteers, set off on the road to London, over 480 kilometres away. Jarrow's M.P., Ellen Wilkinson, led the way. The marchers took turns to carry a heavy oak chest containing a petition which was to be presented in Parliament to Stanley Baldwin, the Prime Minister.

On 1 November the marchers entered London, in a cloudburst, singing to their mouth organ band. They seemed like foreigners beside the better-dressed, better-fed people of the South-East. Next day, while the men sat in the public gallery of the House of Commons, Ellen Wilkinson presented the petition, containing 12,000 signatures. She said:

'During the last fifteen years, Jarrow has passed through a period of industrial depression unparalleled . . . Its shipyard is closed . . .

53

Where formerly 8,000 persons, many of them skilled workmen, were employed, only a hundred are now employed on a temporary scheme. The town cannot be left derelict.'

A short debate followed. Ministers were asked why they could not direct necessary Admiralty orders to Jarrow ship-yards, but no answer was forthcoming. It was a disappointing anticlimax.

The marchers returned from King's Cross by special train. It was 5 November, and they could have been forgiven for sympathising with the intentions of the man who had made the day famous. It seemed as though the whole of Jarrow was out to greet them on their return. The Unemployment Assistance Board provided the only sour note by cutting the 'dole' paid to the marchers. It was explained that while they were away they had not been available for work if any had turned up. Nevertheless, despite the cool reception given them by the Government, the efforts of the marchers were not wasted. They had stirred the public conscience, and that was their real aim.

Gradually new industry came to Jarrow—a steelworks, engineering and ship-breaking—and by 1939 it was recover-ing. But the 'Jarrow Crusade' was not forgotten. It became a symbol of the years of depression and the hardships suffered by 'the army of the unemployed'.

The Jarrow marchers, nearing London

7 No 'Homes for Heroes'

Next to unemployment, housing was the greatest social problem in the 1920s and 1930s. Rows of dismal terraced houses and crumbling cottages—often without baths or inside lavatories—still disfigured both town and countryside. Worse still, there were not enough houses to go round, which caused great overcrowding in the poorer districts of the towns. After the Great War, many workers and their families became increasingly dissatisfied with their living conditions. More and better houses were urgently required. Lloyd George raised everyone's hopes in 1918 when he spoke of 'homes fit for heroes to live in'. However, this promise, like many made after the war, could not be kept in the difficult times which lay ahead.

The Housing Shortage

House-building had for many years lagged behind the growth of population. Pre-war governments, including the Liberals, had done little to improve the situation. They were always reluctant to interfere with private property, unless it was a matter of public health. Where local authorities had used their limited powers, they had been more concerned with knocking down bad houses than building better ones. War increased the shortage. For four years building almost stopped completely while the country concentrated its manpower and resources upon the cause of victory. By 1918 there was a shortage of over half a million houses. This deficit would have to be made up before any further programme of slum clearance could be contemplated.

Whenever things are scarce they become more expensive and the people with the lowest incomes suffer. Housing is no

Family living in one room in the East End of London, 1923

exception. Even before 1914 it was impossible to build decent houses at rents lower-paid workers could afford. They usually had to make do with a couple of rooms or a poky slum. After the war this problem increased, owing to a rise in the cost of materials. It was not so bad for those who could afford to pay more; they still got what they wanted. The real shortage was of houses cheap enough for families with low incomes. As George Orwell said: '"Housing shortage" . . . means very little to anyone with an income of more than £10 a week, or even £5 a week for that matter.' The problem was not confined to the towns. In the countryside, much-needed cottages were not built because the rents that would have to be charged for them were beyond the means of farm labourers.

The Attack on the Housing Shortage

After Lloyd George's rash promise in 1918, Government action seemed essential if poorer families were to have any hope of getting a decent home. Beginning with the Housing Act of 1919, the Government offered subsidies (money grants) to local councils to help them provide homes for families with low incomes. Private builders could also qualify for financial assistance if they built houses which could be let at low rents. In the same year local authorities were instructed to carry out surveys of their housing needs and take action to remedy shortages.

By 1921 the demand from local authorities for housing subsidies was so great that the Government could not stand the cost. The 1919 plan was scrapped. However three years later, in 1924, a Labour Government started a more limited scheme of financial assistance to local authorities to help them build houses working-class families could afford to rent. Significant progress was made in the next ten years, before such subsidies were ended in the National Government's economy drive. Estates of 'council houses' sprang up all over Britain. They were very plain and monotonous to look at; but with gardens, inside lavatories and bathrooms, they were far superior to most previous working-class houses.

Despite subsidies, councils still found it difficult to keep rents low enough. Most of their houses were let to higher paid workers in fairly 'safe' jobs, while the poor and the unemployed had to be satisfied with what they had got. Only just over a quarter of all new houses in the 1920s and 30s were built by local authorities. The rest were mainly sold to private owner-occupiers with comfortable incomes. By the 1930s there were *more than enough* houses in the middle and upper price ranges. The shortage was now entirely confined to cheap, rented accommodation. George Orwell observed that in the poorer parts of towns, 'the mere difficulty of getting hold of a house . . . means that people will put up with anything—any hole and corner slum, any misery of bugs and rotting floors and cracking walls.'

Slum Clearance

Until the 1930s slums were largely ignored by governments. It would have been unwise to tear down existing houses, however bad they were, when there was a serious shortage. By 1930, however, the supply of houses had increased sufficiently for the government to offer a special subsidy to local authorities for slum clearance. The aim was not just to pull slums

57

Typical working-class houses in London, 1925

down, as the Victorians had done, but also to rehouse their inhabitants. To make sure of this, the subsidy was only granted if the slum dwellers were given houses at rents they 'could reasonably be expected to pay'.

In 1933, local authorities were asked to prepare complete programmes for the abolition of slums within five years. Despite great progress in many areas, however, only just over half the work was done by 1939. Lingering on into the 1940s were conditions like these George Orwell found: 'You might walk ... through ... hundreds of miles of streets inhabited by miners, every one of whom, when he is in work, gets black from head to foot every day, without ever passing a house in which one could have a bath.'

Nevertheless, overcrowding was an even greater enemy of health and happiness. It was better to have no bath than to sleep three in a bed. It might have been more sensible if governments had tried to get a separate dwelling for each family before beginning to demolish the slums. Not until 1935 was there a law against serious overcrowding and a five-year plan to abolish it started. Unfortunately the Second World War intervened, and bomb damage put the clock back several years.

Estate of smart, privately-owned houses in Birmingham, 1939

The great burst of house-building between 1919 and 1939 had rehoused almost half the total population. Yet not enough of the right sort of houses were built. Nearly three-quarters were constructed by private builders, most of them for sale to better-off families. By 1939 there were more houses than required for all but the poorest section of the population. Those who were not fortunate enough to get a council house still had to live without baths or inside toilets and often had to put up with overcrowding.

Health Insurance, Pensions and Local Government

Throughout the 1920s and 1930s, National Insurance against sickness remained firmly based on the original scheme of 1911. Rising prices caused the rates of contribution and benefit to be increased, and young workers aged fourteen to sixteen were brought into the scheme in 1937, but otherwise there were no important changes. The wives and children of insured workers were still excluded from free medical attention.

To keep up with the cost of living, pensions were raised to 10s.(50p) a week in 1919. With the proportion of elderly people in the community increasing every year, the cost of pensions to the government was getting out of hand. Up to 1925 they cost more than any other social service, including unemployment benefits. A contributory scheme was therefore introduced whereby people of working age paid a small weekly sum to offset the cost of their pension when they retired. At the

59

same time widows and orphans were also entitled to pensions, for there was still no help except the poor law for families whose breadwinner had died. 'This is the greatest evil and the greatest need of the present time,' said Churchill, now a Conservative Chancellor of the Exchequer, in his 1925 budget speech.

The 1925 contributory pensions scheme was linked with health insurance. The same stamp card was used to record both contributions. The Act which brought the scheme into force was based on the policy of the previous Labour Government. It was the work of Joseph Chamberlain's son Neville, the Conservative Minister of Health from 1924 to 1929. He was a skilful administrator, and the 1925 Act, which, he claimed, completed 'the circle of security for the worker', was only the start of his ambitious programme of reform.

However, the 'circle of security' was far from being complete, as was shown by the large numbers on poor relief in these years. Reform of the poor law was long overdue. Back in 1909 a Royal Commission had suggested that it should be abolished and its functions handed over to the local authorities. This was partly achieved by Chamberlain's Local Government Act of 1929. The Boards of Guardians were at last disbanded, and poor relief was renamed Public Assistance and taken over by the county and county borough councils. The cost of relief could now be spread over a wider area. At the same time the county councils were given bigger grants and extra responsibilities for roads, town planning and child welfare.

Education and Child Welfare

When the Great War ended, expansion of state education was an essential part of Lloyd George's dream of a 'new Britain'. The President of the Board of Education, H. A. L. Fisher, regarded education as 'the most fundamental of all the social services', and, largely through his efforts, an Education Act of 1918 opened the way to future progress. The minimum school-leaving age was fixed at fourteen. It was hoped to continue part-time education beyond fourteen, but lack of money ruled this out almost from the start. Education grants to local authorities were cut by a third in 1921. For most young people, education after fourteen would have to be at 'night school'. The Act also extended medical attention from the elementary to the secondary schools, and restricted the employment of schoolchildren to little more than newspaper rounds and the like.

Secondary education expanded fairly rapidly after the Fisher Act. Meanwhile the curriculum was gradually widened to include science, handicrafts and physical training. But serious inequalities remained. Unless they were very clever, working-class children remained at elementary school until they left at fourteen. On the other hand, unless they were of very low intelligence, children from well-to-do homes went to grammar school, or some other kind of fee-paying school, until they were sixteen or eighteen.

In 1926 a special committee under Sir Henry Hadow recommended secondary education for all, as a right not a privilege. The Hadow Report criticised 'all age' schools. It suggested separate infant and junior schools, to be followed by either grammar or senior elementary schools, depending upon the 'different interests and abilities' of the pupils. Children would be transferred at eleven. '. . . not merely to a different type of teaching within the same school, but to another institution, with a distinctive staff, and organised definitely

A primary school class, 1925

for post-primary education'. These proposals were widely accepted by local education authorities, and by 1939 about two-thirds of the resulting reorganisation was complete. The Hadow Report also recommended a school-leaving age of fifteen. After many delays, an Act bringing this about was prevented from coming into operation in September 1939 by the outbreak of the Second World War.

Ever since the school meals service started in 1906, it had been accepted that state education included more than just teaching. School medical services continued to play an important part in raising the general level of children's health. School meals, where provided, helped to relieve some of the strain of mass unemployment on children. However, even by 1939, less than half of all local education authorities provided solid meals. A Milk Act (1934) made it possible for children to have a third of a pint a day at a reduced price, or free if they could not afford to pay anything.

Welfare services for children below school age were very uneven in distribution and quality. They still depended largely upon local initiative—by go-ahead local authorities or voluntary organisations. The demand for nurseries was increasing, as more women than ever before took full-time jobs, but they remained in short supply. At the end of the 1930s, only about 10 per cent of children under five attended a nursery. There were two main kinds. Day nurseries took the children of working mothers and provided milk, meals and medical attention, and nursery schools and nursery classes in elementary schools were broadly educational in aim.

Perhaps the most important infant welfare service was provided by health visitors. They advised mothers of infants on ordinary day-to-day matters of health, hygiene and child-care. Despite a shortage of staff in many areas, 97 per cent of all children born in England and Wales in 1938 were visited at least once. A similar function was performed by maternity and child welfare clinics. They advised mothers on the feeding and general care of babies and young children and often provided extra services such as vaccination, immunisation and the sale of cheap health foods. When the war came in 1939, priority was given to a further expansion of welfare services for mothers and children.

8 Poverty and Progress in York, 1936

It is now time to return to the city of York and take another close look at working-class life through the eyes of Seebohm Rowntree. In 1936, Rowntree carried out a second survey of the living standards of York's lower-paid citizens. By comparing his findings with those of 1899, he hoped to calculate the extent to which people in a typical English city had benefited from over thirty years of state welfare services. As he rightly said, since his first investigation of 1899 'more far-reaching steps had been taken to raise the standard of life of the workers than during any previous period of similar length.' At the same time Rowntree hoped to highlight the remaining causes of poverty and so point the way to future social reforms.

Seebohm Rowntree

Below the Poverty Line

Every family whose chief wage-earner was paid less than £5 a week was investigated by one of seven interviewers. More than 55,000 people came into this category. To make a comparison with 1899 possible, a poverty line was calculated in the same way. After carefully considering the minimum amount of food, clothing and fuel necessary for the meanest existence, Rowntree arrived at a figure of 30s. 7d. (£1.53), excluding rent, for a family of five. This was adjusted, as before, to fit different-sized families. It was a very bare standard of life, with nothing to spare for things like railway or bus fares, newspapers, letter-writing or smoking and drinking.

Rowntree found 3,767 people living below the poverty line—nearly 4 per cent of the total population, which was now about 90,000. He made no attempt to calculate the number of people who had sufficient income but were in poverty through unwise spending. Therefore the comparative figures from the two surveys in the table below only refer to what Rowntree called 'primary poverty'—people whose income was too low for the barest existence, *even if they spent every penny wisely*.

	1899	1936
Numbers in poverty	7,230	3,767
Percentage of total population in poverty	9.9	3.9

This was a great improvement in such a short space of time. Nevertheless investigation revealed some appalling details. One family of five, all out of work, was found to be living on bread and margarine alone for more than half of each week. This was in spite of unemployment assistance and a widow's pension. A girl of sixteen was prevented from getting work in a factory because she had no respectable clothing to wear. Most of the families in poverty had pawned or sold furniture to pay some of their debts. An old lady of seventy-two, living alone, had no bed and had to sleep on an old sofa. After paying her rent and buying a bag of coal, she had 3s 3d(16p) a week for all her other needs.

A York back-street in the 1930s—houses due for demolition

The Causes of Poverty

In 1899 more than half the poverty had been due to low
wages. This was still a factor in 1936, but only in about one
case in ten. Long-term unemployment now accounted for
almost half the total of those in poverty. Obviously the 'dole'
fell short of what was needed. Temporary unemployment
could usually be overcome by running up debts and by frequent visits to the pawnbroker, but when weeks turned into
months, and months into years, severe poverty resulted.
Rowntree disagreed with those who said the unemployed were
lazy. He estimated that three-quarters of them were 'looking
eagerly for work'.

Poverty in old age had also increased since 1899, in spite of retirement pensions. However the proportion of old people in the community had nearly doubled since the turn of the century and they were now more independent. Many preferred to live alone in poverty rather than become a burden on their children. Nevertheless the state pension could hardly have been sufficient since a fifth of the total in poverty were old people. Even a married couple both drawing a pension required some extra form of income to raise them above the poverty line. Hardship in old age is especially distressing because there is so little chance of things ever getting better. Rowntree was very disturbed to find in his survey so many old folk who were 'pinching, scraping . . . just waiting for the end'.

The aged and the unemployed already received most of their income from the state. The way to raise them out of poverty was simply to increase existing rates of benefit and assistance. However a more difficult problem was presented by large families which suffered poverty even though their fathers had regular jobs. The social services gave little or no help to these people. Rowntree, along with many other reformers, thought 'family allowances', based on the number of children in the family, should be paid by the state to overcome this kind of poverty. Wages were not related to family size, so it was possible for families above the poverty line to drop below it if additional children were born. Clearly, the time extra money was needed most was when the children were young. Rowntree showed that, apart from pensioners, young children had more chance of living in poverty than any other age-group—nearly half of all those in poverty in 1936 were under fourteen years of age.

In addition to family allowances, Rowntree again suggested a minimum wage as a way of removing poverty. Calculating on 1936 prices, it would have had to be at least 53s. (£2.65): 'To keep a family of five in health on 53s. a week . . . needs constant watchfulness and a high degree of skill on the part of the housewife.' He calculated that if a minimum wage of 53s. and a family allowance of 5s. for each child had been in operation in 1936, over 98 per cent of poverty among *families* would have been removed.

An early council estate in York

Housing, Health and Education

York City Council had taken great advantage of government housing subsidies, having itself built more than half of all the new houses since 1920. As a result, the standard of workers' houses had greatly improved and there was much less over-crowding. Over a third of the working population now lived in comfortable, healthy houses—nearly all of them better than the very best had been in 1899. Then, baths and gardens had been almost unknown in workers' houses, but now about a quarter had both. Although the number of slums had been halved, they still made up 10 per cent of the total of houses. Had it not been for the Second World War, Rowntree estimated that 'the slum evil would practically have ceased to exist by 1945'.

Facilities for education compared favourably with those in other cities. As suggested by the Hadow Report, 1926, children went to primary schools until they were eleven, when they took examinations in English and Arithmetic to decide which kind of secondary school would suit them best. The grammar and other selective secondary schools charged fees, but very poor parents did not have to pay. They could even get a maintenance allowance to help them keep their children at school beyond the leaving age. For those who left at fourteen, there was plenty of day continuation and evening education available. Even so, there was still plenty of room for improvement. Classes of forty or fifty were common and many schools lacked changing and washing accommodation. Recreational facilities were poor, with only four playing fields available to 12,000 elementary school pupils.

On the whole, people were healthier than they had ever been. School clinics and free milk and meals for poor children were helping to produce a stronger and fitter younger generation. Better food and improved sanitation helped to prevent disease, so that the overall death rate had halved since 1899. The ill-fed, overworked people of 1899 had little energy for anything. Now people lived a fuller life. Working hours had been reduced from about fifty-four to between forty-four and forty-eight a week since the turn of the century. Holidays with pay were being introduced.

With more leisure and better health, people now took part in a wide range of activities. York had swimming baths and sports clubs, dance halls, a theatre and a music hall. Even the most common entertainments, the cinema and wireless, had been unknown in 1899. For those who wanted to get out and about, there were cheap railway excursions, although many preferred cycling or, if they could afford it, motor-cycles and even cars.

There had certainly been a great improvement in the living standards of working people since 1899. Better wages and smaller families helped, but the main reason for the improvement was the growth of the social services. The workhouse, still important in 1899, was now almost empty. Nevertheless, to know that there had been twice as much poverty at the end of the nineteenth century hardly made that which remained any more tolerable for those who suffered it. As Rowntree said: 'If instead of looking backward we look forward, then we see how far the standard of living of many workers falls short of any standard which could be regarded as satisfactory.'

PART THREE: 'FROM THE CRADLE TO THE GRAVE'

9 Evacuation

On 3 September 1939 Britain once again found herself at war with Germany. The six years of worldwide conflict which followed were to have a vitally important effect on the growth of the British Welfare State. The government was forced to reconsider the whole range of social services in the light of the strain put upon them by the war. Urgent reforms were found to be necessary. Some were carried out at once; others were included in the plans for postwar reconstruction. At the same time, a new sense of unity grew up among the people as they faced together the threat of invasion and conquest. They resolved to break with the years of depression and succeed where their fathers had failed, in building a better Britain when peace returned.

The Second World War involved civilians just as much as the armed forces. The rapid advance of the aeroplane as a weapon of war meant that the bombing of enemy territory was now an important part of military strategy. In these circumstances, the safety and welfare of the people at home had to be considered as well as the needs of the armed services. Plans were made in advance to move families away from areas close to probable air-raid targets into country districts where they would be much safer. The evacuation, as it was called, was the first stage in the 'war on the home front'.

A Window on Town Life

The danger spots which were evacuated were mostly the dockland areas of the major ports and the centres of vital war industries like munitions and aeroplane manufacture. Places such as Glasgow, Liverpool and East London were therefore affected. As it happened, a large proportion of the remaining

Young children being evacuated from London to the West Country

slums in Britain were in these areas, so the evacuation provided a window through which the most squalid aspects of town life could be seen. During the first three days of September 1939 roughly 1¼ million people were evacuated, most of them children. Further movements brought the total up to about 3 million by 1941.

Most of the evacuees were clean and respectable, especially those from areas which had avoided the worst effects of unemployment. However, a less pleasant picture was presented by evacuees from the slum districts, particularly the children. It was the end of the school holidays, and many of them had been running wild for over a month. Their arrival in the countryside was not, therefore, a very good advertisement for town living. Country hostesses had good cause to be shocked by the condition of some of the evacuees they received into their care.

The countryside itself was not free from poverty, but homes were generally in a better state of repair, and dirty, ragged children much rarer. One of the first things to strike people in the reception areas was the poor physical condition of many of the evacuee children. Large numbers were infested with

70

vermin, mainly head lice. These are flat, grey-white insects which lay white eggs, called 'nits', cemented to the hair near the roots. School medical services had long been fighting the problem of lice, and had largely stamped it out in the country areas. However it was still the scourge of the poorer parts of industrial towns.

Head lice were especially common among girls and children under school age. The records of one clinic during the evacuation showed that two-thirds of a party of 320 London schoolchildren were infested with nits on arrival. Even after two or three years' evacuation, children were often re-infested if they visited their homes, and their heads had to be cleansed afresh on their return. Not only nits, but ringworm, impetigo, scabies and a host of other skin disorders were found. They were caused partly by bad housing conditions and lack of hygiene, and partly by ignorance. Some evacuee children and their parents claimed that lice were perfectly natural and saw no cause for concern.

Life in the slums had not encouraged the formation of good living habits. Many evacuee children were not used to using a lavatory. Even up to the age of fifteen or so, they thought nothing of relieving themselves in the street or on a sheet of newspaper. Country hostesses complained bitterly at having to wash clothes soiled through failure to use toilet paper and sheets fouled by frequent bed-wetting. Bad habits even extended to eating. Slum children often had no desire for wholesome food at regular meal-times. Instead, they clamoured for fish and chips, bread and jam, pickles, biscuits, sweets and ice cream.

'Evacuee stories' were soon spreading across garden fences and along shopping queues. The newspapers picked up some startling tales of poverty and neglect uncovered by the evacuation. They told of clothing which was so rotten it had to be cut off and burnt, or of children sewn into a single piece of calico, with a top coat as their only other clothing. Liverpool was nicknamed 'the plimsoll city' in the early months of the war because so many of its evacuated children had no proper outdoor shoes. Worse still, there were children without underwear, nightclothes or even a change of clothing of any kind. Some little girls had never worn pants in their lives.

71

A Turning Point

The living conditions revealed by the evacuation shocked the more fortunate section of the population. Many of them had assumed that, after more than thirty years of state social services, the 'Two Nations' had passed completely into the pages of history books. But the scar left by the depression was deeper and uglier than many thought possible. Some simply shook their heads disapprovingly at 'the way the other half lived', but, when the first shock had passed, an increasing number of better-off people felt a sense of shame at the state of their society.

It was easy to blame parents for neglecting their children. Country folk were understandably annoyed at having to buy clothes for evacuee children while all their parents sent them was sweets and comics. However the time had come to stop criticising and do something positive to raise the living standards of these people. Bad housing was a root cause of many of the problems revealed by the evacuation. It was almost impossible to train children in clean habits when houses, and even some schools, had no indoor lavatories, washing facilities or proper water supply.

One bad thing leads to another. Even sitting down to a family meal is unpleasant in a room several people have slept in. Not surprisingly, children preferred fish and chips in the open air. In these circumstances regular eating habits were never formed, with an obvious effect on health. Noisy, damp and overcrowded slums, with bed-bugs and irritating skin diseases to put up with, made sound sleep impossible. Consequently many children went to school too tired to learn and adults found it difficult to do a good day's work. One little evacuee said of the country: 'I feel so well and happy here; I think it must be the lovely long sleeps we get.'

The remedies were not simple ones. A decent home for every family was the greatest need, along with expanded schemes of National Insurance and medical care for all. It was not just a case of filling a few gaps in the existing social services; a whole new approach was necessary. Material help alone was not the answer. Education, in every sense of the word, was essential. People needed guidance and to have better standards held up to them. Even to begin on such a task would require more far-reaching reforms than had ever been attempted before. However, in the spirit of wartime Britain nothing seemed impossible.

By the summer of 1940, with invasion expected hourly, a new sense of social purpose arose in Britain. The war was a great leveller. Never before had every man, woman and child—rich and poor, at home or overseas—been so exposed to the dangers of enemy attack. When German air-raids began in August, continuing through the winter nights of 1940–41, the people became even more united in their resolve to stand together and resist. In response to the high-pitched whine of the air-raid siren, they crowded together in communal shelters. Social barriers were removed, as people of all classes felt the effects of bomb damage, rationing and shortages, and conscription into the armed forces.

Warfare and Welfare

In May 1940 an all-party Coalition Government was formed under Winston Churchill. Labour Party leaders worked alongside Conservatives in the War Cabinet, and all the bitter political struggles of the 1930s were put aside in face of a common foe. The social services took on a new significance when the 'emergency' came. As the familiar props of everyday life collapsed, the Government found itself forced to step in. Maintaining the morale of civilians 'on the home front' was vitally important. After all, one of the main objects of German air attacks was to try to break the spirit of the British people and bring them to the point of surrender.

City of London workers pick their way through rubble from destroyed buildings, 1940

Mr and Mrs Winston Churchill inspect air-raid damage in London, 1940

During the evacuation, money had been distributed secretly to local education authorities to help them deal with serious cases of neglect that came to their attention. Children in reception areas who needed medical care were given it free of charge. Soon help was needed on a much wider scale by families of dead servicemen, expectant mothers whose husbands were abroad, elderly people cut off from their relations, and the young children of women working in the essential industries. Those on fixed incomes, like pensioners, suffered greatly from a rapid rise in prices after the outbreak of war. The Government immediately introduced supplementary (extra) pensions for old people and widows in 1940. If they had insufficient to live on, they could now apply for extra allowances. Over a million pensioners took advantage of the scheme, showing the widespread need that existed.

Supplementary pensions were paid out of the funds of the Unemployment Assistance Board, which was renamed the Assistance Board in keeping with its wider functions. The means test was eased so that assistance could be given to all who needed it—a further indication of the Government's new attitude. From now on, social services were to be available to all who had need of them, not just the poor. School milk and meals, vitamin foods and milk for infants, and a host of other services were provided for the people as a whole. As well as distributing cash, where needed, the Assistance Board also provided home helps for the sick and elderly. Through helping bombed-out families and others in distress the Assistance Board did much to remove the memory of its earlier association with the hated means test. This was just the beginning of what was to amount to a social revolution in the next few years.

10 Sir William Beveridge

The existing social services had been established at different times without any kind of overall plan in view. Frequent changes, as in the case of unemployment assistance between the wars, only led to further complications. There were different rates of benefit for the sick and the unemployed, even though their needs were similar; more than one contribution card was necessary, and a whole host of government departments were in charge of separate funds for similar purposes. The Coalition Government filled in some gaps, but these emergency measures, however necessary at the time, only led to greater confusion in the long run. Small wonder that many people did not know whether they were entitled to any benefits or not.

It was clearly time to make a thorough investigation of 'social security' in particular, to see if a more logical and complete system could be planned. In June 1941, the Government ordered a special Committee of Inquiry to undertake 'a survey of the existing national schemes of social insurance . . . and to make recommendations'. The chairman of the committee was Sir William Beveridge. No one was better fitted for the task. He had a greater knowledge of social insurance than any other man of his time, and a rare grasp of the difficulties that faced ordinary people in their lives. He was given sole responsibility for settling the contents of the report and signing it, although he was to work with a team of eleven hand-picked civil servants, all experts in different fields.

Beveridge aimed to reconstruct social insurance so as to make all the parts interlock, like the pieces of a jigsaw puzzle. Only by fitting everything into a single plan could the gaps be eliminated and overlapping be avoided. There could be no better time for making a fresh start. As Beveridge said: 'Now, when war is abolishing landmarks of every kind, is the opportunity of using experience in a clear field. A revolutionary moment in the world's history is a time for revolutions, not for patching.' All interested bodies were consulted, including the trade unions, friendly societies and several industrial insurance companies. In all, over forty sets of witnesses were called. Even social surveys, including Seebohm Rowntree's investigation of 1936, were carefully considered. At the end of 1942 the Report was ready. Despite its length (200,000 words, or six times longer than this book) and its complicated calculations, the basic proposals were few, simple and clear.

The Beveridge Report

Beveridge proposed a complete system of insurance covering *all* citizens, whatever their income. Everyone of working age would pay a single weekly contribution, recorded by a stamp on a single card. Employers would continue to pay part of the cost of their employees' stamps. Men would need to pay more than working women, for housewives were to be covered by their husbands' insurance.

Sir William Beveridge—architect of the Welfare State

In return for contributions, flat rate benefits would be paid to all citizens on 'interruption of earnings'—sickness, unemployment or retirement. There would be no time limit on benefits: 'they will continue indefinitely . . . as long as the need continues.' The actual weekly rates would depend on a calculation of the minimum income necessary. So benefits were to be based on a 'national minimum'—a standard of decent living below which no one should be allowed to fall. In addition, there would be extra grants for the normal incidents of life which demanded extra expenditure—maternity grants on the birth of children and a funeral grant.

This was the basis of Beveridge's suggested replacement for all the bits and pieces of insurance and pensions that had accumulated since 1908. It was a simple redistribution of income, achieved by a 'pooling of risks' of the whole community. No means test would be necessary. All citizens would be equal members of the scheme, with an equal right to draw benefits. Beveridge suggested a single new Ministry of Social Security to organise the plan—a great simplification of the arrangements then in force. Because the whole plan was firmly based on the principle of insurance, the state would not be involved in enormous expense. However, the government would be expected to stand the full cost of family allowances. These were to be paid weekly to parents for each dependent child. Beveridge said these family allowances were essential because wages were never related to the needs of a growing family.

The insurance scheme was not a complete system of social security. It dealt only with *want*, and, as Beveridge said, 'Want is only one of the five giants on the road of reconstruction and social progress.' The other 'giants' were *disease*, which would require a new health service, 'securing medical treatment of all kinds for all citizens'; *ignorance*, which could only be overcome with 'more and better schools'; *squalor*, which meant 'more and better houses' so that every family had a decent home, and *idleness*, or unemployment. This could only be kept in check by government action to stimulate trade and industry. Beveridge said that if pre-war governments had concentrated on making sure there was enough work, they would not have had to patch the holes in insurance with the 'dole'.

The Beveridge Report was the most important single influence on the making of the Welfare State. Although the approach was original, most of the contents were already familiar. Apart from family allowances, the death grant and the principle of applying insurance to everyone, the plan was firmly based on the foundations of 1911. It simply rounded off all that had gone before. As Beveridge said: 'The scheme proposed is in some ways a revolution, but in more important ways it is a natural development from the past.'

Public Approval

On 2 December 1942 the newspapers set out the details of the finished plan. It was received by the public like a new gospel. Long queues formed outside His Majesty's Stationery Office, where the Report was on sale. Official literature had never been so eagerly read. The Report was a best seller from the start, and before long well over half a million copies were sold.

Beveridge had succeeded in capturing the spirit of the times, and he became a national hero overnight. As an American commentator put it: 'Sir William, possibly next to Mr Churchill, is the most popular figure in Britain today.'

Soldiers overseas were equally eager to get information about the Report. The plan to abolish want gave them something to fight *for* as well as against. Beveridge was well aware of this need. He said of his proposals: 'They are a sign of the belief that the object of government in peace and in war is not the glory of rulers or of races, but the happiness of the common man.' The Army Bureau of Current Affairs produced a pamphlet on the Beveridge Plan for distribution among soldiers. Even the Americans wanted to read about it. The Treasury made a profit of $5,000 from sales of a special United States edition of the Report.

As with all plans for reform, there was criticism of the Report. Some dismissed it as being too ambitious. Others feared that it gave *too much* security, so that people would no longer have to 'save for a rainy day'. The most common criticism was that the inclusion of all citizens in the insurance scheme and family allowances would mean that well-to-do people would draw benefits they did not need. But most people felt that this was one of the strengths of the plan. Everyone had a right to claim benefit, so there was no need for a means test and no suggestion of poor relief about it. The principle of a 'national minimum' standard of living could at last be achieved.

The critics were in a small minority. On the whole there was overwhelming agreement that the Beveridge Plan should be put into effect. 'Social security from the cradle to the grave'—this was the new Britain that people wanted. Beveridge himself was left in no doubt about the public reception of his Report. He was approached in the street by people who wished to thank him personally. An old age pensioner from Plymouth sent him thanks in the form of a verse:

> At last there is a saint on earth;
> An angel he would be
> If only he could have his will
> And make the Commons pass his bill.

Government Caution

As the pensioner's verse indicated, there was not yet any promise from the Government that the Report would become law. True, they had commissioned Beveridge to undertake the task, but he was only asked to make recommendations. Whether the recommendations were acted upon was another matter. In a radio broadcast, Beveridge warned people not to take the Government's attitude for granted:

'What I have been telling you is simply my proposals to the Government. The Government are not committed in any way to anything that I have said. They've only just seen my Report and you won't expect them to make up their minds . . . without full consideration.'

Beveridge during a campaign of speeches, 1943. (He was not a good public speaker, but at this time he could fill any hall in Britain)

In fact, Churchill and his Cabinet were in a difficult position. They thought they had ordered a technical survey of social insurance which could be used as a basis for reform but did not commit them in any way. Instead they were presented with a fully fledged programme of reform, carefully worked out to the last detail. The great publicity it was given and the public acclaim it received embarrassed the Government still further. It seemed that they were the only people in Britain who had not made up their minds about the Report. After the failure of the promises following the First World War about 'a land fit for heroes', they were anxious not to raise false hopes this time. So they delayed making definite plans until they had taken a long, careful look at the Report.

The Beveridge Plan was debated in the House of Commons for three days in February 1943, but the Government refrained from making any promises. An official spokesman said it was 'bold and imaginative' and that the financial situation at the end of the war would determine what could be done. A motion in favour of the Report was carried by 335 votes to 119. A month later, Churchill, in a broadcast, promised a four-year plan of reconstruction after the war, but he also warned against too much talk of peace while the war was still raging. He did not think it fair to tell 'fairy stories' about the future. Meanwhile, the Beveridge Report was being considered by a committee of officials in Whitehall. Eventually, in 1944, a new scheme of social insurance was prepared. It was firmly based on Beveridge's plan, although, as we shall see in Chapter 12, some important adjustments were made.

11 Child Welfare and Education

In the early years of the war, before the Beveridge Report became the centre of attention, great advances were made in the care of children. From the evacuation, which revealed so much neglect, right through the heavy bombing of 1940–41, the needs of the young always came first. The Government did all in its power to combat ill health and undernourishment among children. Not only physical needs were met. Before the war was over, the whole state system of education was reshaped for the future in the Act of 1944.

Infant Welfare

One of the most disturbing things brought to light by the evacuation was the poor state of health of many children below school age. They were often the worst affected by skin disorders and other marks of bad living conditions. The Government therefore decided to give top priority to the care of infants and their mothers. But they no longer thought in terms of helping just the poorest families. The shortages, mishaps and dangers of war were shared by the whole population, and it was the Government's duty to protect the health and well-being of every child, rich or poor.

A National Milk Scheme was started in July 1940. All children under five and expectant and nursing mothers were entitled to a pint of milk a day for twopence (1p)—less than half the full price. If the family income was below £2 a week, the milk was given free. National Dried Milk for babies was soon offered as an alternative. The entire cost of the subsidy was met by the Government, for, as Churchill said: 'There is no finer investment for any community than putting milk into babies.' By the end of the war there were nearly 4 million consumers of subsidised milk, and the scheme was continued in peacetime.

By 1941 the effect of the war on foreign trade was causing concern about the nation's diet. Imported fruits such as oranges had almost disappeared from the shops, and there was a danger that expectant mothers and young children might suffer from a deficiency of vitamin C. The Ministry of Health acted quickly. Cod-liver oil and blackcurrant extracts were made available, free of charge, at welfare centres and food offices. Early in 1942 National Rose Hip Syrup, a valuable source of vitamin C, appeared in chemists' shops, reserved mainly for young children. This was produced in large quantities by a remarkable campaign. Throughout the summer and autumn of 1941, women's and children's organisations, including the Scouts and Girl Guides, scoured the hedgerows for rose hips. They picked about 200 tonnes in all—enough to employ nine firms in making the syrup.

Before long, concentrated orange juice was obtained from the U.S.A., and this gradually replaced the blackcurrant products. The milk and vitamin food schemes had already been merged, and a small charge was put on the vitamin

A child receiving essential foods from the 'Hand of War'

foods. By the end of 1942 all children under five and expectant mothers were supplied with subsidised milk, cod-liver oil and orange juice. 'Now here surely is a fact to give the utmost encouragement and hope to all of us', said the *Daily Mirror*. 'In the midst of war, Great Britain is able to build better children's bodies than in times of peace.'

After the war, when fresh fruit and other sources of vitamins reappeared on the market, the scheme was not so essential. Nevertheless, when family allowances were introduced (1946) milk and vitamin foods were continued as part of the weekly benefits. Even today, milk and vitamins can be obtained from child health clinics at a reduced price, or in certain circumstances free of charge.

When regular night bombing began, in the autumn of 1940, people were forced to crowd together into air-raid shelters. In these conditions all kinds of infection could be passed on, not least among them diphtheria—the most dangerous of children's diseases. Consequently the Ministry of Health began a campaign to have children immunised against diphtheria. Leaflets, posters and advertisements in newspapers and magazines all warned parents of the danger. By the end of the war, half the nation's children had been immunised and no serious epidemic had occurred. Deaths from diphtheria in

Baby being weighed at a welfare clinic, 1944

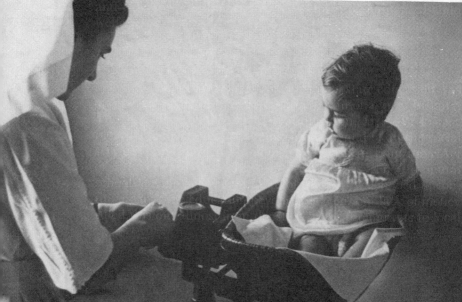

Britain had numbered nearly 3,000 in 1938. By 1945 the total was down to 720. In contrast, deaths from the disease mounted in most other European countries during the war—especially in Germany.

The war put a great strain on the existing infant welfare services, especially in the evacuation areas. At first, many welfare centres had their buildings taken over by Civil Defence units, and health visitors were often needed for other tasks. But gradually extra staff and buildings were found and the number of welfare centres was greater at the end of the war than at the beginning. Voluntary workers played a very important part in these services and also in the much needed expansion of nurseries. The Government was eager to get more married women into the essential industries, so some local authorities were given extra financial help to provide nurseries. As a result more young children were taught, where necessary, good eating and sleeping habits and bodily cleanliness—things which had been found seriously lacking in many evacuee children.

School Milk and Meals

Before July 1940 school meals had been little more than a form of poor relief, to be provided for very undernourished children. But the war brought about a complete change of

Children serving their own school dinners

Mid-morning milk break

policy. With many mothers going out to work, there was a need for midday school meals for children from all kinds of homes, not just the poor. In any case, the Government was concerned with the possible effect of food shortages on children's health and wanted to ensure that they all got a good meal at midday. Local education authorities were therefore encouraged to extend their meals service. An official report said: 'There is no question of capacity to pay. We may find children of well-to-do parents and the children of the poor suffering alike from an inability to get the food they need.'

After a year, the number of subsidised school meals being provided had doubled. The same attitude was taken over school milk—there was a 50 per cent increase in the amount consumed during the same period. In September 1941 it was decided to provide milk for *all* schoolchildren at a subsidised price, although the poor continued to get theirs free. The *Daily Mirror* later commented: 'Not so long ago hundreds of thousands of children of the poor never drank fresh milk. Now each child has at least half a pint a day.'

These services continued when the war ended. Until 1968 a third of a pint of milk was given to all children free of charge. Similarly, meals at subsidised prices were made available to all who wanted them, and given free in cases of special need (see page 129). In the late 1940s well over half of all pupils in state schools had their midday meal at school. Parents had no hesitation about using a service which was freely available to everyone, regardless of income.

Education and the 1944 Act

Throughout the war years, educational reform was a frequent topic of discussion. The future of Britain's schools was bound to be an important part of the plans for peacetime reconstruction. Broadcasting to the nation in 1943, Churchill stressed the importance of giving every child the fullest educational opportunity: 'We must make sure that the path to the highest functions throughout our society and empire is really open to the children of every family.'

The urgent need for skilled workers during the war revealed serious gaps in the education system—especially the sorry state of technical education. Churchill reminded the people that the future of the world was in the hands of 'the highly-educated races, who alone can handle the scientific apparatus necessary for pre-eminence in peace or survival in war. . . . You cannot conduct a modern community except with an adequate supply of persons upon whose education much time and money have been spent.'

In 1944, under the guidance of R. A. Butler, President of the Board of Education, a new Act brought together all the plans for educational reform in England and Wales. (The Scottish system had always developed independently and required separate Acts of Parliament.) 'Free secondary education for all' would be the basis of the post-war system. The reorganisation suggested by the Hadow Report of 1926 (see page 61) was to be completed, with some important additions. The idea of 'elementary' education disappeared completely and was replaced by three progressive stages—primary, secondary and 'further'. Nursery schools would also be provided for younger children. The leaving age was to be raised to fifteen almost immediately, and to sixteen as soon as possible after that. Physically and mentally handicapped children were not left out. It was the duty of local education authorities to provide suitable schools for all children according to 'age, aptitude and ability'—and milk, meals and medical services as well.

In future, children would leave primary school at 'eleven-plus'. In practice this meant that those who were successful in an examination would proceed either to a grammar school, with an academic curriculum, or, where provided, to a technical high school, with a bias towards applied science. The remainder (about 75 per cent) would go to a 'modern' school, where the emphasis would be on practical subjects.

It was intended to provide three years of part-time further education for fifteen-year-old leavers at 'county colleges', but lack of money killed this plan. Instead, day release classes at colleges of further education were expanded, to give young people technical or commercial training while they were in a regular job. A great expansion of universities was also planned. Local authority grants for full-time study would make it possible for any boy or girl with sufficient ability to progress from school to university without financial help from their parents.

The 1944 Act in Practice

All was ready for a massive expansion of secondary and further education when the war finished. But there were many obstacles in the path of progress. Air-raids had destroyed or damaged 5,000 schools. This, together with a wartime rise in

the birth rate, caused great overcrowding of existing build-ings. Difficulties increased when the school leaving age was raised to fifteen in 1947. There were not enough teachers for all the extra classes. An emergency campaign was started to attract people from all walks of life into special teacher-training courses. Throughout the summer of 1947 posters appealed to people to MAKE TEACHING YOUR CAREER. Meanwhile children were moving into new schools while bricklayers, carpenters and painters worked around them.

Before long the system of selection at 'eleven-plus' began to attract mounting criticism. People said it was unfair to make drastic decisions about a child's future at such an early age. Children often suffered from strain as a result of being 'crammed' for the 'eleven-plus' examination, and in any case there were grave doubts as to whether the examination itself was sufficiently reliable. All three types of secondary school were supposed to be of equal rank and importance, but this was just wishful thinking. Grammar schools were the aim of most parents and children because they provided the surest route to higher education and desirable jobs. Instead of 'deciding suitability for different types of secondary educa-tion', the eleven-plus examination was a simple case of pass or fail—the 'sheep' to the grammar school, the 'goats' to the modern.

The 1944 Act did, however, go a long way towards remov-ing wealth as a direct influence on state secondary education. With the exception of 165 'direct grant' grammar schools, which could still charge fees for half their places, the Act abolished fee-paying in grammar schools. Well-to-do families had previously been able to take a grammar school educa-tion almost for granted because about half of these schools had charged fees before the war. Now it was 'ordeal by eleven-plus' for almost everyone. But private fee-paying schools, outside the state system, continued to flourish. Wealthy parents often sent their children to private schools if they 'failed' the eleven-plus. There they would be able to stay on until at least sixteen and take the new General Certi-ficate of Education (G.C.E.), which replaced the School Cer-tificate in 1951, even if it was only intended for 'academic' children who had passed the eleven-plus.

Some local authorities had doubts about the eleven-plus right from the start. Even as the 1944 Act was becoming law the London County Council voted in favour of 'comprehensive' schools. These would take children of all abilities at eleven and provide suitable courses for them under one roof (see page 127). Primary schools had, of course, always been 'comprehensive'. When London County Council's first brand new secondary comprehensive school—Kidbrooke—was opened in 1954, with room for 1,700 girls and ninety staff, the newspaper headlines gave a clear indication of the great difference of opinion about this type of school. The *News Chronicle*, which has since ceased publication, hailed it as 'THE FIRST PALACE OF LEARNING', while the *Evening Standard* called it a 'SAUSAGE MACHINE'.

The Children Act, 1948

The improvements in child welfare which were either planned or already in operation by 1945 were, of course, primarily intended for children living with their families at home. However, an incident at the end of the war brought sharply into focus the needs of children deprived of a normal home life. A little boy called Denis O'Neill, who was boarded-out on a lonely farm in northern England, was thrashed so brutally that he died. This was not the first case of its kind, yet public opinion was aroused as never before.

A special committee investigated local authorities' arrangements for taking children into care, and revealed some serious shortcomings. In some local authority homes and hostels, normal children were mixed with the mentally defective and with old people. The resulting Children Act (1948) stressed the importance of a family background for deprived children, but made local authorities supervise 'boarding-out' much more strictly than before, to prevent any repeat of the Denis O'Neill incident. Children's Officers would find homes for deprived children and visit them regularly. All homes had to conform with standards laid down by the Home Office. Voluntary organisations, such as the National Society for the Prevention of Cruelty to Children (N.S.P.C.C.) and Dr Barnardo's Homes, continued to flourish in co-operation with the state.

12 Social Security—The Attack on Want

Germany surrendered on 7 May 1945, and Japan three months later, bringing the Second World War to an end. Peace had come at last, and with it the chance to build the 'new Britain' planned during the war. Much had been done already. Infant welfare services and school milk and meals were well established, and the 1944 Education Act had begun the attack on the first of Beveridge's 'five giants'—*Ignorance*. Before the remaining 'giants' could be tackled, however, there would have to be a general election, the first for ten years, to decide which party was to take on the task of reconstruction.

'The Labour Landslide'

The Coalition Government was broken up in May 1945, having achieved its war aims. For the next few months, Churchill and the Conservatives remained in office until an election could be held. Churchill had ambitious plans of his own for tackling the problems of reconstruction, including a massive house-building programme. Most people expected his war record to carry him to victory at the polls. Imagine the surprise when, on 26 July, the following result was announced: Labour—393 seats; Conservative—198; Liberal and Independent—32. The Labour victory was even more decisive than that of the Liberals in 1905. Like the result forty years before, the 1945 election heralded a period of far-reaching social reform.

The election result was not intended to be a rejection of Churchill's achievements as a war leader. He was a national hero, and when he died in 1965 he was honoured as no Englishman had ever been before. One main reason for the Conservative defeat was simply that people wanted to break with the past—the days of 'dole' queues and the means test. Labour had been in power for less than three years throughout the 1920s and 30s, so they could hardly be blamed for the miseries of the Depression. A Conservative M.P., Christopher Hollis, later said of the election result: 'However we may have voted in 1945, none of us looking back can deny there was at that time a general feeling of disgust in the nation, just or unjust, with the past.'

The new Prime Minister, Clement Attlee, and his Cabinet, faced a mammoth task. The enormous cost of fighting the war had left Britain heavily in debt. Large areas of several major towns and cities had been reduced to rubble in the air-raids. Food, clothing and fuel were strictly rationed, and almost everything was in short supply. There could hardly have been a more difficult time to try to set up a Welfare State. But the people were determined that nothing should be allowed to hold back the tide of social reform. 1945 was not a time for excuses or delay.

Clement Attlee in July 1945

Family Allowances

The heart of the Beveridge plan was 'social security'—the attack on the 'giant' *want*. This would be achieved largely by National Insurance, but family allowances were an important part of the overall scheme. They had already become law in 1945, before the election, although the first payments were not made until August 1946. The arguments in favour of family allowances put forward by Beveridge, Rowntree and many others had proved unanswerable. Because wages were not related to family size, the arrival of each child lowered the standard of living of the whole family. Since the idea of a national minimum wage had failed to gain acceptance, family allowances were the next best thing. They ensured that extra money went *at the right time* to those who needed it.

Beveridge had suggested a weekly allowance of 8s. (40p) for each child, but Churchill's Government fixed it at 5s. (25p) for each child *after the first*, up to the age of sixteen or the start of full-time employment. It was given in the form of a book of coupons, to be cashed at a post office. The Government justified the smaller sum of 5s. on the grounds that welfare foods and school milk and meals had been expanded to a far greater extent than Beveridge could have foreseen. By shifting a proportion of the allowance on to these services, the child was ensured of getting some of the benefit directly. Allowances were not given for the first born because it was assumed that the family income would be sufficient to stand the cost of one child without hardship. It was never intended that the state should take over the responsibility of parents to provide for their children. The cost of child-rearing would in future be shared between the parents and the community as a whole.

Family allowances were not based on insurance contributions, so the entire cost came out of national taxation. Any family could qualify for them, regardless of income. This was criticised because many families did not need the extra money. However the basic principle of the new social services was that they should avoid means tests as far as possible. So every family was treated alike, although, in practice, the poorest ones gained most from family allowances because they did not have to pay income tax on them. The rates of allowances

93

were increased from time to time, and from 1956 third and additional children received more than the second. In the same year the age limit was raised to eighteen for children in full-time education.

National Insurance

After some delay, the Coalition Government accepted most of Beveridge's proposals in 1944, and a new Ministry of National Insurance was set up. The Labour Government carried on with the wartime plans, and National Insurance became law in 1946. The Act differed from the Beveridge Report's proposals in one very important respect. It was not based on a 'national minimum' standard of living. This would have required automatic adjustments to meet changes in the cost of living, and the Government considered such an arrangement too complicated. They preferred to fix rates of benefit by Act of Parliament and review them periodically. But as it turned out benefits failed to keep up with rising prices and soon fell a long way behind minimum needs.

A National Insurance Card

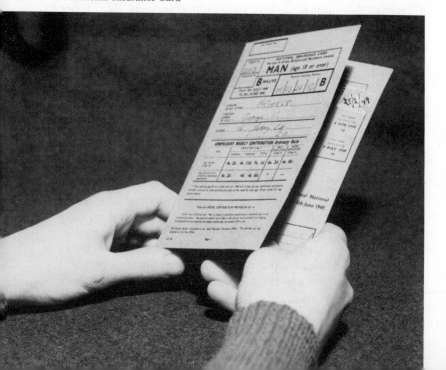

National Insurance was compulsory for everyone of working age except married women. Rates of contribution varied according to whether people were employed, self-employed or unemployed. Lower scales of contribution and benefit applied to young people under eighteen. Benefits were paid for 'interruption of earnings', caused by sickness, unemployment or old age. However, if earnings were lost through taking part in a strike, benefit was not paid. It was up to the trade unions to provide their members with 'strike pay'. Benefits could also be withheld if claimants refused to take any suitable job that was offered them by the labour exchange. Pensions were paid on 'retirement'. Old people were encouraged to work beyond the normal retiring age of sixty-five (men) or sixty (women) by an addition to the basic rate of pension for each year it was deferred. When the scheme began, two-thirds of the men and half the women who qualified for a pension decided to continue working.

There were other benefits stemming from the weekly contribution. Maternity grants were given to mothers—a lump

A new employment exchange, 1949. Compare these comfortable surroundings with the 1910 labour exchange pictured on page 40

sum paid on the birth of each child. If the mother had previously been working and had paid enough contributions, she got an additional allowance for eighteen weeks from her own insurance. Then there was the death grant, to help with funeral expenses, and widows' pensions and guardians' allowances. A separate, but linked, scheme was introduced by the Industrial Injuries Act (1946). It dealt with compensation for those injured, disabled or killed at work and those suffering from industrial diseases.

The weekly contribution for an employed person—4s. 11d. (24½p) when the scheme started—was a smaller proportion of the average wage than the amount deducted today. James Griffiths, Minister of National Insurance, said the scheme was 'the best and the cheapest insurance policy offered to the British people, or to any people anywhere'. Speaking for the Opposition in Parliament, R. A. Butler said: 'I think we should take pride that the British race has been able . . . shortly after the terrible period through which we have all passed together, to show the whole world that we are able to produce a social insurance scheme of this character'.

The running of the scheme was a vast undertaking. The records of every insured person were kept in the central offices of the Ministry of National Insurance, which were built on the outskirts of Newcastle. *The Times* explained the scale of this operation: 'Each insured person has his own ledger-sheet on which his whole insurance life history can be recorded; and there are similar records for the family allowance scheme. The 25,000,000 sheets of the insurance ledger are located in 100 different rooms, each of which is occupied by a staff of twenty.' Everyone had a National Insurance number. This was simpler than using names, especially if the name was Smith. There were 650,000 members of the Smith family in the scheme—8,000 of them called John Smith!

National Assistance

Not all citizens are normally healthy or reasonably fortunate. Some people need looking after even though they have not paid for it through insurance. They include the blind, deaf, crippled, mentally handicapped, deserted or unmarried mothers and the wives and children of criminals. The National Assistance Board was established in 1948 to help these people. It was the disguised descendant of the Poor Law. The cost of poor relief, which had once fallen on the parish, was now, through national taxation, spread over the whole population. Among its many duties, the Assistance Board had to provide reception centres for the homeless, where they could be trained for re-entry into employment, and old people's homes, run by local authorities.

The Assistance Board also provided a 'safety net' for those whose needs were not fully satisfied by National Insurance benefits. It was hoped that it would not have an active future in this respect, but the reverse happened in practice. The failure to relate insurance benefits to a minimum standard of living meant that the 'safety net' was soon bulging. Most of those in need of extra help were old people, who found that their pension was not enough to live on. Beveridge himself pointed out with regret, in 1953, that a quarter of all those receiving retirement or widows' pensions had to go to the Assistance Board for more money. The proportion would have been higher still if everyone in need had applied. However, many old people were too proud to ask for what they regarded as charity.

National Assistance was available to anyone over sixteen who could give evidence of being in need. It was therefore necessary for applicants to undergo a 'needs test'. This was

An applicant for National Assistance undergoing a 'needs' test

different from the old means test, however, because the incomes of other members of the family did not have to be declared. The whole service was very personal and each case was treated on its merits. The Board could give weekly cash donations, lump sums for things like tools for a job, and even allowances of clothing or bedding, if needed. The Board's calculations were based on certain minimum standards of living (like Rowntree's poverty line, although a little more generous). So the 'national minimum' idea was not entirely lost.

'Full' Employment

The Second World War gave employment to jobless workers and so brought to an end the years of depression (see Chapter 6). Nevertheless Beveridge warned that his whole scheme of social security could collapse if mass unemployment—the 'giant' *idleness*—returned after the war. He urged the Government to take whatever action might be necessary to maintain a high level of employment in peacetime. Ways of doing this had been put forward before the war by John Maynard Keynes, a Cambridge University lecturer.

Keynes pointed to the simple fact that money spent by one person is earned by others and then re-spent, over and over again. In other words, one person's spending is, at least eventually, someone else's work. This operates the same way in reverse. If, say, £100 is *not* spent, the consequences become magnified as it is *not* earned by other people, *not* re-spent and so on. This had happened during the depression. Many people were out of work because there was *not enough spending altogether* by individuals, businesses and governments. Too little spending led to lower production, less earned in wages, even less spending and so on in a downward spiral.

Beveridge accepted Keynes's argument that the government should be prepared, where necessary, to boost the total amount of spending. When an industrial depression threatened, firms could be given special incentives such as reduced taxes or lower interest rates to encourage them to spend on new factories and equipment. Above all, the government could increase its *own* spending—on social services, armaments and 'public works' such as roadbuilding. The result

John Maynard Keynes

would be more people at work, more wages earned and profits made by businesses. These extra wages and profits would be spent and so encourage further increases in production.

Such thinking had a big influence on politicians during and after the war and led to a reversal of pre-war policies. In 1944 all parties in the Coalition Government pledged themselves to try to maintain 'a high and stable level of employment' in the future. Whenever there were signs of a coming depression, the government would borrow money and increase its spending, on services and public works, to 'prime the pump' and get industry expanding again. (This was the opposite of the National Government's policy, in the 1930s, of *cutting* its spending to keep a balanced budget). Future governments would also encourage the building of new factories in depressed areas and help redundant workers to learn fresh skills.

'Full' employment was now the aim. However, this does not mean that *everyone* willing and able to work has a job. There are always some people 'between jobs' or being retrained in new skills. In 1945 it was thought that 'full' employment would mean keeping the unemployment rate down to about 3 per cent of the total labour force (the average figure between the wars was 13 per cent). In practice, the

Percentage of working people unemployed 1920–1970

average from 1945 to the early 1970s was only about 2 per cent. An overall expansion of world trade was a vital factor in keeping the wheels of industry turning. But the 'Keynesian' policies of successive governments also played an important part. This curbing of unemployment meant there were fewer claimants for National Insurance than expected. But the picture began to change in the 1970s (see page 132) as the jobless total mounted alarmingly and the system of social security came under severe pressure.

13 Health and Housing

The attack on the two remaining 'giants'—*disease* and *squalor*—was spearheaded by Aneurin Bevan, who, as Minister of Health, 1945–50, was responsible for both health and housing policy. The creation of a free health service was one of his greatest ambitions. His father had been a founder member of the Working Men's Medical Aid Society in Tredegar, Monmouthshire, and, in his earlier life, Aneurin Bevan had seen ill health and squalor in abundance. Now was his chance to do something about it. The National Health Service, his biggest task, probably captured the imagination of the public more than any other reform of these years. It came into operation on the same day as National Insurance and National Assistance—5 July 1948.

Aneurin Bevan—at the Ministry of Health, 1945

'The Appointed Day'

On the evening of Sunday, 4 July 1948, Mr Attlee spoke to the nation on B.B.C. radio. The subject of his broadcast was the official beginning of the Welfare State on the following day. The public was already well informed about the new services—largely through a stream of explanatory leaflets and family guides. The Prime Minister could therefore concentrate on matters of wider importance. He was particularly anxious to stress the all-party origins of the social services, rightly refusing to take all the credit for his own party. Lloyd George and Beveridge, who had prepared so much of the ground, were Liberals, and most of the reconstruction plans had been made under a Conservative, Winston Churchill, while leader of a Coalition Government.

Mr Attlee explained that the quality of the new services would depend on the amount of money the country could afford to spend on them. So it was up to everyone to work hard to increase the national income, for 'the general level of production settles our standard of material wellbeing'. The country's finances had not yet recovered from the war, and

there were some, like the writer of a *Daily Mail* editorial, who advised a postponement of some of the Government's plans until Britain was back on her feet. But most people would not hear of any delay. The *Daily Mirror* summed up their feelings on 5 July:

'THE DAY IS HERE! For years the reformers of all parties have tried to safeguard the aged, the poor and the sick. Much has been done—much more than in any other large country. But always YOU wanted fuller protection against misfortune. You wanted the State to accept larger responsibility for the individual citizen who served it faithfully. YOU WANTED SOCIAL SECURITY. FROM THIS DAY HENCE, YOU HAVE IT.'

The National Health Service in the Making

Like the other main services of the Welfare State which began their active life on the Appointed Day, the National Health Service was the result of wartime experience and planning. In 1939 the state health service was still basically that created by the Liberals in 1911 (see Chapter 5). There had been growing public dissatisfaction with its shortcomings, especially the exclusion of the wives and children of insured workers from free medical treatment. The doctors themselves were not satisfied with 'Robin Hood medicine', which meant overcharging the rich in order to cover the cost of treating the poor free. Changes which had been contemplated for years without result were suddenly forced upon the government by the war.

In 1938, fearing the outcome of German aggression in Europe, the Ministry of Health began to plan emergency medical services. Arrangements for the reception of air-raid casualties were especially important. To get some idea of what was needed, a survey was made of all hospital facilities. It revealed an overall shortage of hospital beds of about one-third—allowing for the prospect of heavy war casualties. Many hospital buildings had been developed from Victorian workhouses. They had old-fashioned wards and equipment in ugly, prisonlike buildings. To make matters worse there was a grave shortage of nursing staff. With no time to spare, the government set about providing additional beds, either in

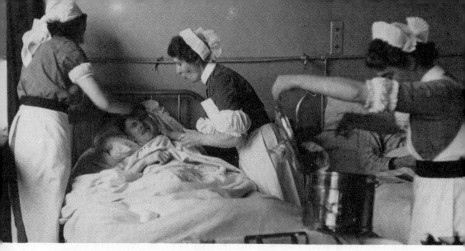

Red Cross nurses in a wartime hospital

existing buildings or in converted annexes and huts. Equipment was also improved. Nearly 1,000 new operating theatres
were installed by October 1939.

The supply of doctors and specialists demanded equally
urgent attention. They normally preferred to practise in pleasant, residential areas where most people were fairly well off.
This was the best way of making sure they got their bills paid.
Industrial towns, particularly in the depressed areas, were
much less attractive to doctors, with their high proportion of
poor patients. There were seven times more doctors per head
of the population in Kensington, a well-to-do area of London,
than in South Shields, in the heart of the depressed North-
East. In view of the emergency, however, the government was
forced to interfere and transfer some doctors and specialists
from desirable districts to the 'undoctored areas'.

The practical experience of war preparations revealed the
urgent need for a full-scale state health service. It also provided an opportunity for experimenting with different methods of achieving it. Early in 1944, the Coalition Government
produced a plan for a National Health Service which would
be 'free to all' and financed out of national taxation:

'Just as people are accustomed to look to public organisation for
essential facilities like a clean and safe water supply . . . so they
should now be able to look for proper facilities for the care of their
personal health to a publicly organised service available to all who
want to use it.'

104

The National Health Service Act

Labour took over the Coalition Government's plan, making some important changes in it, and the National Health Service Act was passed in 1946. The whole range of medical treatment, including the services of dentists and opticians, was to be provided free to everyone. People would not be compelled to use the state services. Doctors and patients who wished to continue with private practice were free to do so, but the aim was to make the state service so attractive that all would want to use it.

The hospital services were completely remodelled. The Coalition Government had not intended that they should be taken over by the state, but Labour, true to its principle of nationalisation, took all but the teaching hospitals into public ownership, under the Ministry of Health. Bevan had been strongly opposed to voluntary hospitals. He said medical care should not have to rely on charity—nurses should be looking after the sick, not selling flags. Nevertheless, the voluntary spirit was not entirely lost in the new service. The National League of Hospital Friends was soon busy helping patients with things like shopping, and raising money for extra items such as television sets, telephone trolleys and bed curtains, which hospital management committees could not always afford.

A national system of general practitioners—G.P.s—was provided. To ensure their even distribution over the whole country, the Medical Practices Committee would draft new applicants to the 'undoctored areas'. Both doctors and patients would have a free choice. Patients could change their doctor if they wished, and doctors could refuse to take certain patients on their lists. If people fell ill while away from home, they could call in any National Health doctor. All this varied little from pre-war days, except, of course, that everyone was now included and there were no bills to pay.

County and county borough councils would provide midwives, home nurses and health visitors, and were responsible for vaccination, immunisation and the provision of ambulances. These services had normally been provided before but they had not previously been compulsory. A completely new idea, stemming from the wartime plan, was the introduction of local authority 'health centres'. In these, G.P.s would work together, with the latest equipment, and would be able to call in the skills of the specialist when required. This would lead to greater efficiency, for, as a British Medical Association report admitted, 'the days when a doctor, armed only with his stethoscope and his drugs, could offer a fairly complete medical service are gone.'

The National Health Service Act was one of the most far-reaching reforms in parliamentary history. Yet the scheme was nearly wrecked by the violent opposition of the doctors. Two months before the Appointed Day, two out of every three doctors voted against joining the service. They did not oppose the *principle* of a free health service for all, but they objected strongly to some of the details of the Act. They feared that the Government was trying to restrict their freedom and give them too little say in organising the new services. Bevan refused to give way on major issues, although he did make some minor concessions to the doctors' demands—over things like the way they would be paid. An uneasy truce was established, just in time for the service to begin as planned. Ever since Lloyd George's scheme of 1911, doctors have been very sensitive to state control and ready to assert their rights if they feel that any government is trying to restrict their freedom and responsibility.

The Stampede

'One would think the people saved up their illnesses for the first free day.' The comment of one G.P. probably summed up the feelings of thousands of others when the National Health Service began. Surgeries were invaded like bargain sales. The 'family doctor' service, so long out of reach of many people, was at last a reality for everyone, and they rushed to make use of it. Dentists, too, were in great demand. They were soon booked solid many months ahead, and there was even a five months' wait for spectacles from opticians. Before long, Bevan had to appeal to the public to use the National Health Service sensibly.

This was immediately seized upon by critics of the scheme.

A crowded doctor's waiting room in London shortly after the start of the National Health Service

They said the health service was an encouragement to people who wanted something for nothing and that taxpayers' money was being needlessly squandered. However, the Government was quick to point out that much of the pressure on the health service resulted from pre-war neglect. In 1939, for example, about 6 million people needed spectacles but did not have them. It was common practice for people to test their eyes in Woolworths and buy a pair of glasses for $6d(2\frac{1}{2}p)$. The nation's teeth were also suffering from neglect. Local authority clinics found that a majority of women had at least half their teeth decayed or missing. Small wonder, said the Ministry of Health, that there was such a stampede for the new services.

In any case, the scheme was not being run for the benefit of the poor alone. Most middle-class people were very grateful for it too. Medical care had recently become very expensive for everyone. A G.P. commented: 'The local aristocracy have joined the National Health Service; they wait their turn in the surgery with the rest.' This was just what Bevan had hoped for. As he said when the scheme started, 'we want everyone in, from the millionaires to the poorest.' Although some private practice continued, well over 95 per cent of all doctors and patients joined the state scheme. Only 6,000 'pay beds' were needed for private hospital patients, out of a total of over 240,000 beds.

Mothers with babies wait to see the doctor at a mobile health centre —Ruislip, Middlesex, 1953

In terms of money and manpower, the National Health Service became the second largest undertaking in the country—next to the armed forces. Nevertheless, there were still acute shortages of staff and equipment. Health centres, which were intended to be the heart of the new health service, were still rare twenty years after the Act was passed. The first one was not opened until 1952, at Woodberry Down, London. Five years later there were still less than twenty in the whole country. Without health centres, the hospitals had to take on an increasing burden and queues of outpatients got longer. Lack of money for new hospitals meant that hundreds of dreary, old-fashioned buildings still had to be used.

The great pressure on the National Health Service, and the soaring costs which resulted, soon led to the introduction of charges for some of the services. Part of the cost of dentures had to be paid, and £1 was charged for each course of dental treatment for those over twenty-one. Prescription charges were also imposed, together with a contribution towards the cost of spectacles, although schoolchildren could still get free spectacles if they had standard frames. Bevan, then Minister of Labour, resigned from the Government in 1951 as a protest against these charges. He said they were against the principle of a *free* health service.

108

The Problem of Housing

In 1945 the housing situation was desperate. For six years building had almost ceased, while in the same period nearly a third of all houses were damaged or destroyed by bombing. Even without war damage, more than 500,000 new houses were needed just to replace the worst slums. This was the size of the problem facing Aneurin Bevan, for until the formation of the Ministry of Housing and Local Government (1951) housing was the responsibility of the Minister of Health. An emergency housing drive was essential, but, before this could begin, temporary accommodation had to be found for the homeless. Aircraft factories were turned into prefabricated dwellings, and whole colonies of new 'prefabs' were built—a continuation of the Coalition Government's policy. Even then, many small houses had two families living in them.

"*Well, were you or were you NOT the young couple advertising for a roof to put over their heads?*"

109

Bevan concentrated on building subsidised council houses for renting. Private building for sale could only be carried on under licence and was severely restricted. This ensured that most of the resources of the building industry were put into the Government's housing drive. Bevan was not prepared to accept second-rate houses, thrown up in a hurry. Despite the emergency he insisted that council houses should be good ones, with a natural life of about eighty years. They were expensive, but he refused to reduce standards. Even though materials were in short supply, Britain produced 1 million new houses in the first five years after the war—more than any other European country.

The Government was criticised for favouring the working classes in its housing policy, but Bevan was determined to give priority to those whose needs were greatest. Gradually, as the shortage was reduced, council housing became more classless, like the other social services. A Housing Act of 1949 showed this change of attitude. Local authorities were to provide for *all*, not just the 'working class'. By the 1950s a wide cross-section of society occupied council houses, many of them with well-paid jobs and expensive cars. People who thought of council housing as a special service for the poor objected to this. They said it was unfair to give subsidised houses to people who could afford to pay the full rent. As time went by fewer people seemed prepared to accept the idea that housing should be a social service for all, in the same way as schooling or medical care.

In the ten years after the war, three-quarters of all new houses were built by local authorities and new town development corporations. By then a quarter of the total population lived in publicly owned property. However an Act of 1956 reflected the different priorities of the Conservative Government of the time. It discontinued all subsidies to local authorities, except those for slum clearance and the building of new towns. From then on, private house-building accelerated once more. An increasing number of people began to borrow money from building societies and buy their own homes—although prices were too high for house purchase to be within the reach of lower-paid workers, especially in London and the South-East.

New and Expanding Towns

A New Towns Act (1946) combined the need to build more houses with the task of reducing overcrowding in the main centres of population. New communities were to be established close to London and other big cities to take their 'overspill'. The land would be bought by compulsory purchase, and local authorities would receive government subsidies to help them build houses for renting. Work on the first twelve new towns began by 1950. In the next thirty years, twenty more were planned and started—bringing the total to twenty-three in England and Wales, five in Scotland and four in Northern Ireland. By then (1980) new towns housed over 2 million people. Planners were given opportunities to put new ideas into practice. Things like traffic-free shopping centres, the separation of industrial zones from residential areas and improved traffic control are easier to achieve in a town which is carefully planned as a whole before a brick is laid.

Blocks of flats going up and already occupied, Harlow New Town, Essex—1951

The new towns of Britain in 1980

Another experiment stemmed from the Town Development Act, 1952. The government decided to assist the expansion of existing small towns which were willing to take some of the population from overcrowded cities. Worsley, in Lancashire, had already begun to take the overspill from nearby Salford before the Act was passed, and Wolverhampton and Walsall had made similar arrangements before 1952. Bletchley, Aylesbury and Swindon soon followed, and a number of other 'expanded towns' were planned for the future.

New housing and land planning were closely linked. Under the Town and Country Planning Act of 1947, all councils were required to submit a 'development plan' for government approval. Any scheme could be blocked if it looked like producing ugly or haphazard 'urban sprawl'. By the mid-1950s, although many housing problems remained, especially in decaying inner city areas, the 'giant' *squalor* was beginning to assume much smaller proportions.

14 Poverty and the Welfare State in York, 1950

All the main services of the Welfare State had been established by 1948. Soon afterwards Seebohm Rowntree completed his series of investigations into poverty in York. He was, naturally, interested in finding out '. . . how far the various welfare measures which have come into force since 1936 (the date of the previous survey) have succeeded in reducing poverty'. By confining our attention once more to York, we can get a close-up view of what the social services meant to ordinary people.

Poverty and the Social Services

As before, Rowntree began by calculating a 'poverty line'. In addition to food, clothing and necessary household expenditure on things such as fuel and lighting, he added a small allowance for 'personal sundries'—travel, wireless licence, newspapers, postage, stationery and so forth. By 1950 the general standard of living had risen so much that it was unrealistic to leave out these items. In fact, things like drink and cigarettes were rarely cut out altogether in times of hardship. They were merely reduced and some more essential items were cut down as well. Consequently it was always difficult to draw a satisfactory poverty line; people rarely spent all their money sensibly. Nevertheless, leaving out rent and rates, Rowntree estimated that £5 0s. 2d. (£5.01) was the minimum weekly income necessary for a family of five. This was again adjusted to fit all family sizes, including single people living alone.

Instead of interviewing every working-class family in a population of 105,000, Rowntree arranged to have a sample taken of one house in nine where the main income of the family was below £10 10s. 0d. (£10.50). Such sampling methods were used satisfactorily in all kinds of social investigations by this time. On the basis of his research, Rowntree calculated that 1,746 persons were living in poverty—1.6 per cent of the whole population. We are now in a position to summarise half a century of social progress in one simple table, but, before we do so, there are two important points to remember. First, these figures are only for 'primary poverty'. In other words, they take no account of people who had enough income but became poor by spending some of it unwisely. Second, the 1950 figure would have been lower if it had been based on the same standard of living as those for 1899 and 1936. The 1950 poverty line was a good deal more generous.

THE REDUCTION OF POVERTY, 1899–1950

	1899	1936	1950
Percentage of the total population in poverty	9·5	3·9	1·6
Main cause of poverty	Low wages	Unemployment	Old age

As the table shows, old age had become the main cause of poverty by 1950. In fact, it accounted for more than two-thirds of the total. The retirement pension was clearly insufficient to live on. Many old people were receiving supplementary pensions from the National Assistance Board on top of their basic pension, yet they still could not make ends meet. Some cases of hardship found among pensioners were more typical of the 'bad old days' than of the mid-twentieth century. An old man of seventy-six said he had no money for replacement of any household goods or clothes. His only material pleasure, a small tin of tobacco a week, had to be given up for several weeks when he had his shoes repaired. Another pensioner said: 'These clothes will have to last until I die; I shall never be able to afford any more.' Nevertheless, many expressed gratitude for the new scheme of social security. Before 1948 they had lived on less. If the Welfare State had not abolished poverty altogether, it at least seemed to have reduced its amount and severity.

Perhaps the most remarkable discovery in the whole survey was the fact that not a single family was in poverty through unemployment. The reason was not that National Insurance

115

Seebohm Rowntree found that old age was by far the most common cause of poverty by 1950

benefits were sufficient on their own, although they were much more substantial than before, but that the few who were out of work had some form of extra income in addition to unemployment benefit. The high level of employment which had been maintained during the 1940s had obviously played a great part in reducing poverty. Rowntree observed that if mass unemployment returned, on the scale of the 1930s, it would have a marked effect on the numbers in poverty. He calculated that if 8.8 per cent of the workforce had been unemployed (which had been the figure in York in 1936) the number of poor would have more than doubled.

Housing and Health

By 1950, four-fifths of all houses in York were classed as 'satisfactory'. The other fifth were planned for demolition by 1967. Overcrowding had virtually disappeared, although proper bathrooms were lacking in almost half the houses occupied by working-class families. Considering the effect of six years of war on the housing programme, York City Council had made great progress since 1936. Well over a fifth of

116

all the houses in the city were council houses. The government subsidies paid on them were an important part of the benefits of the Welfare State. Rowntree concluded: 'We do not suggest that . . . everybody now has adequate accommodation, on the contrary, many rooms are dark and small, particularly in the houses scheduled for demolition. . . . But the fact remains that substantial progress has been made since 1936.'

It was not possible to calculate accurately the value of the National Health Service. Its benefits were difficult to measure—although there could be no doubt that most families had gained immensely from the wide range of medical services now freely available to them. The fact that on average children of all ages were taller and heavier than they had been in 1936 gives some idea of the general improvement in physique.

AVERAGE HEIGHTS AND WEIGHTS OF SCHOOLCHILDREN, 1936–50

		Average Weight	Average Height
Children from families *just above* the	1936	30·38 kg	132·08 cm
poverty line	1950	31·52 kg	132·71 cm
Children from 'middle-class'	1936	33·78 kg	136·52 cm
families	1950	34·46 kg	137·79 cm

The expansion of child welfare services since the outbreak of the war had contributed to these improvements.

The Task Not Yet Complete

This third survey of York was published in 1951—the year of Rowntree's eightieth birthday, and three years before his death. He could look back on a lifetime which had spanned the most remarkable social progress in British history. The York of 1899 had changed out of all recognition. However, the reduction in poverty was not entirely due to the social services. More married women were working in 1950 than ever before, and their extra income often made the difference between poverty and a comfortable standard of living. Also, the survey was carried out at a time when there was hardly any unemployment. Without these two factors, living standards would have been much lower for many families.

117

New flats in York, opened 1951 by the Duchess of Gloucester

There was, after all, still hardship. The problem of poverty had become largely a problem of old age. Pensions had never been sufficient to live on and they were now falling behind the cost of living. With the proportion of elderly people in the community increasing yearly, this was an urgent problem. Many old people were too proud to go to the National Assistance Board and ask for what they regarded as charity. After the survey was completed, in 1951, pensions were increased. Rowntree calculated that if this had been done before his investigation it would have halved his figure for the total numbers in poverty. This showed how important it would be in the future to keep pension rates in line with rises in the cost of living.

118

15 New Directions in the Social Services

In the period 1940–48 social services were for the first time planned and created as part of an overall scheme. The achievements of these years were spurred on by the Second World War. It drew together the whole community in face of a common danger and kindled a desire to combat the kind of distress and hardship that had been felt by millions of families in the 1920s and 30s. As Beveridge said in his Report, 'War breeds national unity. It may be possible, through a sense of national unity . . . to bring about changes which . . . it might be difficult to make at other times.'

Social Security or Santa Claus?

As the wartime spirit of social reform began to fade, criticisms of the Welfare State were heard increasingly. It was said that the British would become spineless and lazy, that their initiative and ambition would be sapped by having social security, medical care and the rest 'served up on a plate'. In July 1948, *The Times* asked: 'Can the next generation reap the benefits of a social service state while avoiding the perils of a Santa Claus State?' Many believed that such 'perils' could not be avoided—a viewpoint illustrated by the *Punch* cartoon on page 120, which dates from 1949.

It is true that many people, especially of the younger generation, came to *expect* the state to look after their interests. The same people would often grumble about taxes and National Insurance contributions without stopping to think how everything was paid for. But this did not necessarily take away their ambition. After all, the aim of the Beveridge scheme was '. . . not that of a Welfare State providing everything that the citizen could desire. The idea was that of a

THE WELFARE STATE

minimum guaranteed by the state.' It was assumed that individuals would use their abilities to the full to achieve 'something above the minimum'. In this way, initiative and drive would still be needed to secure a good standard of living.

An American critic once said to Beveridge that if there had been social security in the days of Queen Elizabeth I there would probably have been no Drake, Hawkins or Raleigh. Beveridge replied that *these* great Elizabethans had had social security from birth: 'Adventure came not from the half-starved, but from those who were well-fed enough to feel ambition.' In the sixteenth century 'freedom from want' was a privilege enjoyed by a small section of society—as it was even 300 years later during Victoria's reign. Beveridge wanted this freedom extended to every citizen as a birthright.

'Casualties' of the Welfare State

While critics went on claiming that the Welfare State made life too easy for people, evidence began to emerge that, in some respects at least, the reforms of the 1940s had not gone far enough. Indeed, poverty and hardship seemed to be

120

increasing. It was calculated in 1954 that 8 per cent of the population (4 million people) were living on or below the official 'poverty line' of the National Assistance Board.

Who were these 'casualties' of the Welfare State—the millions in need who found that the state did *not* in fact provide a reasonable minimum standard of living? Seebohm Rowntree had discovered, in his third survey of York (1950), that poverty was mainly a problem of old age. At that time more than two-thirds of those living below the poverty line in York were pensioners (see Chapter 14).

From the start of the National Insurance scheme in 1948, cash benefits—which of course included pensions—were set lower than Beveridge had recommended. Moreover their value declined as they failed to keep pace with rises in the cost of living. In the 1950s and 60s this did not worry most people of working age because of the very small amount of unemployment. But retired people who could not manage on their pension and had no other source of income needed to apply for National Assistance—renamed Supplementary Benefit in 1966. Unfortunately many old people did not claim the extra money because they considered it 'charity'. They preferred to remain in poverty and keep their self-respect. In 1963, while 2½ million people were receiving National Assistance, a further 1 million who were entitled to it did not apply.

Large families, too, often became 'casualties' of the Welfare State, especially if they depended on just one wage-earner in a low-paid job. What Rowntree had found back in 1936 was still true: that young children had more chance of being in poverty than any other age group apart from pensioners. Family Allowances had been introduced to ease this problem, but, as with National Insurance, they failed to keep up with rising prices. There was clearly a need to bring the system of social security more into line with the needs of the poorest groups in the community.

Social Security: the Selective Approach

Advertisements were put in newspapers and on TV to encourage pensioners and other people in need to claim all the money to which they were entitled. To the same end, the old

Cash help

you can claim supplementary benefit if you are:

over pension age

or

bringing up children on your own

or

too sick or disabled to work

or

only able to work part time

or

looking after a disabled relative

The Department of Health and Social Security has to advertise to encourage all those who are entitled to Supplementary Benefit to claim it

system of social security was reorganised. A new, unified Department of Health and Social Security (D.H.S.S.) was set up in 1968, bringing together National Insurance, Supplementary Benefit (the new name for National Assistance) and aspects of the Health Service. Enquiries about the whole range of benefits could now be dealt with in one office. It was hoped that those who had previously been reluctant to advertise their poverty by going to the old Assistance Board would now seek help. But over half a million old people who qualified for a Supplementary Pension still did not claim it.

To help low-paid workers with large families, the rates of Family Allowances were increased in 1968—for the first time since 1956. Most of the extra money went to parents with four or more children. But it was still not enough. Some low-paid workers found they were actually better off if they gave up their jobs: their National Insurance and Supplementary Benefit (which included allowances for children) amounted to more than they could earn.

One of the benefits of the FIS scheme is free school meals for the claimant's children

To encourage such people to go on working, the Family Income Supplement (F.I.S.) was introduced in 1971. Low-paid workers (including single parents) with at least one child can claim weekly cash allowances on top of their wages—the amount depending on their income and the size of their family. They can also claim free school meals for their children and other benefits, including free dental treatment, spectacles and medical prescriptions. However benefits can be lost if the wage-earner's income rises above F.I.S. levels. So the scheme gives the low-paid little incentive to increase their earnings. Its critics called it a 'poverty trap' and pointed out similarities with the Speenhamland System of the eighteenth century (see page 8).

Like Supplementary Benefit, F.I.S. concentrates help where it is most needed. However, both go against the basic principles upon which the Welfare State was founded in the 1940s. They are paid out of general taxation, not insurance contributions, and they are *selective* (only available to those who have exceptional needs). But to return to the Beveridge principle of *universal* benefits (available to all, regardless of income) would require massive increases in National Insurance contributions. Rather than do this, recent governments have abandoned the idea of equal treatment for all.

A more selective approach was also applied to National

Insurance. By the late 1950s rapidly rising incomes meant that there was often an enormous gap between people's regular earnings and National Insurance benefits. The retirement pension presented the biggest problem: it was often less than 20 per cent of the earnings of higher paid workers before they retired. Consequently many employers were running *additional* private pension schemes. The time seemed ripe to extend state pensions so that higher paid workers could contribute a little more each week for a larger pension on retirement. The resulting scheme of Graduated Pensions began in 1961. The same idea was applied to sickness and unemployment benefits in 1966. These were related to normal earnings by getting the higher paid to make bigger weekly contributions for larger benefits.

This 'wage-related principle' was taken further in 1975 with a new Earnings Related Scheme. The stamp card was abolished and National Insurance contributions became a *percentage of earnings* up to a certain limit (8.75 per cent of up to £220 per week in 1982–3). At first, higher contributions earned higher benefits, but as the jobless total mounted (see page 132) the cost of unemployment benefits soared. From 1982, only flat-rate benefits were paid to all claimants. Pensions were reorganised differently because two-thirds of all employees now belonged to private schemes run by employers. In 1978 a 'two-tier' pensions scheme was introduced. This consisted of a *basic* pension, equivalent to the old flat-rate one, and an *additional* pension related to earnings. Those belonging to satisfactory private schemes could opt out of the additional state pension.

Meanwhile, a new scheme of Child Benefit replaced Family Allowances in 1977. Until then, the Inland Revenue had made an allowance for each dependant child when calculating the income tax payable by the parents. But the poorest families do not normally have to pay income tax, so they gained nothing. From 1977, these tax allowances for children were gradually withdrawn and the money saved was used to pay enlarged Child Benefit—for *every* dependant child (the first child was excluded from the old Family Allowance scheme). All parents qualify for Child Benefit, and single parents get extra money on top of the basic rate.

Health and Housing: Private versus Public

In the National Health Service (N.H.S.) lack of money has meant continual shortages of facilities. The long awaited health centres were established in most areas by the 1970s, but hospital waiting lists lengthened. In 1949 about half a million people were on waiting lists for hospital treatment; the numbers rose to 600,000 in 1966 and to 800,000 in 1978. To avoid delays, increasing numbers of wealthier people became private (paying) patients, usually covering the cost with medical insurance. The total membership of private medical insurance schemes increased from half a million in 1955 to

The British United Provident Association (BUPA) is the largest organisation in Britain offering private health insurance

over 3 million in 1980. A private patient can usually have a routine operation such as removal of the tonsils almost immediately, whereas an N.H.S. patient might have to wait a year.

Despite attempts to achieve an even distribution of doctors, there were still proportionately more in middle-class areas, especially in southern England, than in working-class districts. Moreover, population shifts to new towns and estates meant that there were often more than enough hospital beds available in inner cities and too few in expanding areas. In many ways the N.H.S. has not lived up to the expectations of its founders. In particular, the move towards a 'double standard' of health care—with better and more prompt services for those able to pay—defeats the original purpose of the N.H.S. Many doctors welcome the fees they earn from private patients, and they enjoy being able to give a more 'personal' service. But opponents of private medicine say it weakens the N.H.S. by diverting staff and other resources away from poorer patients whose needs may be greater.

In housing, there has been a much greater shift of emphasis from public to private. From the mid-1950s onwards, the majority of new houses were built for sale—to 'owner-occupiers', who borrowed most of the money they needed from building societies. The number of owner-occupiers increased from 4½ million in 1950 to 12 million thirty years later. But the need to pay a deposit, usually at least 5 per cent of the cost of the house, to qualify for a building society mortgage (loan) still put home ownership beyond the reach of millions of families.

Meanwhile publicly owned houses for renting continued to be built—many of them in the new towns, which went on increasing in size and number (see map on page 112). By the 1950s and 60s, council houses were often occupied by families with two or more wage-earners and it seemed unfair in such cases that rents should be subsidised. In 1972 a Conservative Government substantially increased council rents, but a 'rent rebate' scheme allowed poorer families to claim back some of their money—another example of the 'selective' approach to the social services. The Conservatives also favour the selling of council houses to their occupants. In 1980 councils were

Among the many homes classed as unfit for habitation some, like the one pictured here, do not have fixed baths

instructed to sell dwellings to tenants of at least three years' standing who wanted to buy them. The Labour Party opposed this policy, saying that there were already too few council houses available for those who needed to rent them.

Since the 1960s the total supply of houses has actually exceeded the number of family units in Britain. But this has not ended the country's housing problems. There were still half a million homes classed as unfit for habitation in 1980, despite massive slum clearance schemes since the war. Furthermore there are often surplus houses in areas of declining industry, where they are not needed, and shortages in expanding areas. The bright hopes of the 1940s have not been realised: in most parts of Britain there are still not enough decent houses which low-paid workers can afford.

Education: Expansion and Contraction

We saw in Chapter 11 that the selection of pupils for different types of secondary school at eleven-plus attracted mounting criticism. Some L.E.A.s (local education authorities) began to scrap eleven-plus selection as early as the 1950s—in favour of comprehensive schools which took pupils of all abilities.

Circular 10/65 which made comprehensive schools official government policy

Meanwhile the number of young people staying on at school beyond the minimum leaving age (then fifteen) doubled between 1945 and 1960. Secondary modern schools developed extended courses to sixteen, entering their brightest pupils for G.C.E. 'O' Level—even though this examination had been designed for the grammar schools. As numbers staying on in secondary modern schools continued to increase, the C.S.E. (Certificate of Secondary Education) was introduced, in 1965, for the majority of pupils.

In the same year, comprehensive schools were made official policy by a Labour Government. Its *Circular 10/65* asked (it did not compel) L.E.A.s to submit plans for ending selection at eleven. Comprehensive reorganisation began in many areas. However, some Conservative-controlled L.E.A.s disagreed with the policy and did not cooperate. The Conservatives gradually came to accept comprehensive schools, although they defended the right of any L.E.A. to choose to keep selection. A later Labour Government took a tougher line in 1976. It abolished the 'direct grant' grammar schools (see page 89), most of which became independent schools charging fees, and tried to compel the few remaining L.E.A.s with selective schools to 'go comprehensive'. When the Conservatives returned to power in 1979 this compulsion was removed.

In 1980, over 90 per cent of state secondary school pupils in the U.K. attended comprehensives—more than double the proportion ten years earlier. By this time the period of rapid change and expansion in the education service was over. The number of pupils in schools was falling sharply (owing to a declining birth rate in the 1970s) and some schools had to be closed. Cuts in government spending on education in the late 1970s and early 1980s led to complaints from teachers that they lacked the resources needed to do their job properly.

Lack of money was not a new problem in education. It delayed the raising of the school-leaving age to sixteen until 1973—nearly thirty years after the 1944 Education Act had stressed the need for this reform. Money was also saved on school milk and meals. Free milk was restricted to primary schools in 1968 and to the under-sevens in 1971. From 1980, L.E.A.s were no longer required to provide any milk; and government control over school meal prices was removed, to allow L.E.A.s to charge more.

For thirty years or so after the war there was a massive expansion of higher education. The number of universities increased from seventeen in 1945 to forty-five by 1979. Some were wholly new. Others grew out of colleges of advanced technology (C.A.T.s), which were created in the 1950s to meet Britain's need for more applied scientists. From the 1960s, polytechnics developed a wide range of degree courses, and teacher training colleges (renamed colleges of education) increased in size and number—until fewer jobs for teachers

The Open University, established in 1971 at Milton Keynes in Buckinghamshire, provides correspondence courses, backed by radio and TV programmes, for those unable to study full-time for a degree

led to many closures from the late 1970s. The number of full-time university students more than doubled in the 1960s. But then the increase in student numbers began to level out and cuts in government spending on universities led to fewer places in higher education in the early 1980s.

Personal Social Services

Some people—particularly the very old, the handicapped and homeless children—often have difficulty in running their own lives. In such cases the state needs to do more than just provide financial assistance. Proper care and attention can only be provided effectively through direct personal contact. This is the job of social workers and other helpers employed by the local council. Such personal social services have developed very largely since the Second World War.

Personal services for the elderly and handicapped are generally designed to help them go on living in their own homes. These include home helps to do the housework, the delivery of cooked 'meals on wheels', day centres, luncheon clubs and

130

'Meals on Wheels'—one of the personal social services provided for old people and the handicapped

special workshops and social centres for handicapped people. In many areas 'sheltered housing' is available for old people. This usually consists of a group of flats or bungalows which are self-contained but have some joint facilities and the services of a warden in case of emergencies. However, some old and physically or mentally handicapped people are unable to live in the normal community, even with special help. Residential homes and hostels have to be provided in such cases.

Since 1971, the whole range of personal services has been organised by the social services department of each local council. Others helped include 'problem families', young offenders and children deprived of a normal home life. All children under seventeen whose parents are unable or unwilling to provide for them must be taken into the care of the local authority. Where possible, they are 'boarded out' with foster parents, who receive a maintenance allowance. Alternatively they are placed in children's homes, some run by voluntary organisations, such as Dr Barnardo's, in co-operation with the state.

The Shadow of Unemployment Returns

In the post-war years it was confidently expected that the new social services would virtually abolish poverty. The British people talked proudly of '*the* Welfare State', as if Britain were the only country which cared for its citizens in this way. In fact all industrial countries had social security and welfare services, and a few had started them before Britain. Moreover, standards were rising faster abroad than in Britain. This was because most of Britain's industrial rivals were expanding their production more rapidly and growing richer much faster. The social services a country can afford depend on its national income, and this, in turn, depends on the productivity of those at work.

Britain's poor industrial performance in recent years is reflected in her social services. People complain about long queues in hospitals and surgeries, lengthening waiting lists for council houses and cuts in spending on education. But extra staff and other resources needed to improve services would have to be paid for out of higher taxation—and this would lower people's living standards in other ways. To make the available money go further, recent governments have made the social services more selective. For instance, council house rents have been increased but poorer tenants given rebates; health service charges have risen except for those entitled to free prescriptions; Supplementary Benefit and F.I.S. are paid only to the poorest people. Such selective services can often be humiliating because claimants have to answer personal questions about their income, but they cost a lot less than 'universal' services for all.

For many years after the Second World War the payout of National Insurance benefits was kept within bounds by the low level of unemployment. But more recently new pressures have been put upon the Welfare State by a massive increase in the numbers out of work. Between 1970 and 1979 the total of unemployed people doubled—from roughly ¾ million to 1½ million. Much worse was to come. In the next two years (1980–81) the jobless total doubled again, officially passing the 3 million mark in January 1982. The Earnings Related Scheme of National Insurance was abandoned, and from 1982

After a lapse of forty years, large scale unemployment returns to Britain

only basic rate benefits were paid to the unemployed.

Although living standards in Britain have fallen behind those in many other industrial countries, the people as a whole are still better off now than ever before. They are on average better fed, housed, clothed, educated and cared for medically than past generations. For millions of people life without the social services would be almost unthinkable. Nevertheless, the highest hopes of the 1940s have not been realised. In 1982, 6 million people were living on or below the official poverty line—more than one in ten of the population—and the number claiming Supplementary Benefit (4 million) was the highest ever recorded. Although there were no longer 'Two Nations' in the Victorian sense, the gulf separating rich and poor was still vast and seemingly unbridgeable.

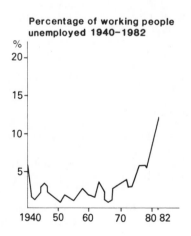

Percentage of working people unemployed 1940–1982

Index

Timeline

1834	Poor Law Amendment Act—workhouses for the 'able-bodied poor'
1848	First Public Health Act
1850	Factory Act—ten-and-a-half-hour day
1870	Education Act—beginning of board schools
1875	Artisans' Dwellings Act—to promote slum clearance
1880	Compulsory elementary education
1890	Housing of the Working Classes Act
1891	Free elementary education
1897	Workmen's Compensation Act
1902	Education Act—beginnings of state secondary education
1905	Unemployed Workmen Act
1906	School meals for poor children
1907	School medical inspection Scholarships to secondary schools—'free places'
1908	Children Act—protection of children, juvenile courts, probation service Old age pensions—non-contributory
1909	'The People's Budget'—graduated taxation Trade Boards—for fixing wages in 'sweated industries' Labour exchanges
1911	National Insurance Act—insurance against sickness and unemployment
1918	Education Act—leaving age fixed at fourteen
1919 1923 1924	} Subsidised Housing Acts—local authority 'council houses'
1920 –21	Unemployment insurance extended to most workers and their dependants
1925	Contributory old age, widows' and orphans' pensions

136